Simply the

BEST JOKE BOOK

Ever!

Diane Canwell

with Jon Sutherland

STAR FIRE

Publisher and Creative Director: Nick Wells
Project Editor: Sonya Newland
Designer: Robert Walster

This is a Star Fire book
First published in 2005

06 08 10 09 07

1 3 5 7 9 8 6 4 2

STAR FIRE is part of
The Foundry Creative Media Company Limited
Crabtree Hall, Crabtree Lane, Fulham, London, SW6 6TY

www.star-fire.co.uk

A CIP record for this book is available from the British Library.

ISBN 1 84451 450 1

Printed in China

CONTENTS

BUSINESS AND WORK JOKES

5-73

CROSS-THE-ROAD-JOKES

75-86

FAMILY AND RELATIONSHIP JOKES

87-162

LIGHT BULB JOKES

163-188

MISCELLANEOUS JOKES

189-256

BUSINESS AND WORK JOKES

A young man was at a job interview. He had completed all the paperwork and sat anxiously awaiting the outcome. After reviewing his forms, a woman from HR called him into her office. 'We do have an opening for people like you,' she said. 'Fantastic,' he replied. 'What is it?' 'It is called the door!'

If clergymen are defrocked, shouldn't it follow that electricians are delighted, cowboys deranged, bed-makers debunked, landscapers deflowered and software engineers detested?

A man calls his doctor. He is frantic. 'My wife is pregnant and her contractions are only two minutes apart,' he shouts. 'Is this her first child?' asks the doctor. 'No you idiot – it's her husband!'

A nurse was showing some student nurses through the hospital. 'This will be the most hazardous section in the hospital for you. The men on this floor are almost well.

A man walks up to the counter at the airport. 'Can I help you?' asks the agent. 'I want a return ticket,' says the man. 'Where to?' asks the agent. 'Right back to here.'

A man telephoned a travel agent and asked,
'How long does it take to fly to Spain?'
The travel agent said, 'Just a minute...'
'Thank you,' the man said and hung up.

A man went to the dentist.
The dentist said 'Say Aaah'.
The man said 'Why?'
'Because my dog's just died,' replied the dentist.

A new manager spends a week at his new office with the
manager he is replacing. On the last day the departing
manager tells him, 'I have left three numbered envelopes
in the desk drawer. Open an envelope if you encounter a
crisis you can't solve.'
Three months later there is a major problem, and everything
goes wrong. The new manager feels threatened, but he
remembers the parting words of his predecessor and opens the
first envelope. The message inside says, 'Blame your
predecessor!' He does this and gets off the hook. About three
months later, the company is experiencing a dip in sales,
combined with serious product problems. The manager quickly
opens the second envelope. The message reads, 'Reorganize!'
This he does, and the company quickly rebounds. Three
months later, at his next crisis, he opens the third envelope.
The message inside says, 'Prepare three envelopes'.

A waiter brings his customer the steak he ordered,
with his thumb over the meat.
'Do you expect me to eat that?' yelled the customer. 'You've
had your hand on it!'
'What?' answers the waiter, 'you want it to fall
on the floor again?'

A coach-load of tourists arrived at Runnymede. They gather around the guide who says, 'This is the very place where the barons forced King John to sign the Magna Carta.'
A man in the front of the crowd asks, 'When did that happen?'
'1215,' answers the guide.
The man looks at his watch and says,
'Damn! Just missed it by a half hour!'

A recently qualified accountant went for a job interview.
The interviewer, the owner and a self-made man,
was very agitated and arrogant.
'I need someone with an accounting degree,
but I mainly need someone to do
my worrying for me,' he says.
'Okay,' replied the applicant. 'What is it exactly
you want me to do?'
'Well I worry about lots of things, but I don't want
to worry about money. Your job will take all those money
worries away from me.'
'I understand. How much does this job pay?'
'I'll start you at £100,000,' replies the businessman.
'That's amazing! How can you afford that? You're only a
small business,' asks the applicant.
'That's your first money worry! Now get to work.'

A man goes into a pharmacist shop and asks whether they can give him something for hiccups. The pharmacist leans forward and slaps the man across the face.
'Why did you do that?' asks the stunned customer.
'Your hiccups are cured aren't they?' replies the pharmacist.
'No, but my wife out in the car still has them.'

A man makes an appointment to see a famous lawyer.
'Can you tell me how much you charge?' asks the client.
'I charge £500 to answer three questions,'

replies the lawyer.
'That's expensive isn't it?' answers the client.
'Yes it is,' says the lawyer, 'what's your third question?'

A man visits his GP and asks for help,
as his hands will not stop shaking.
'Do you drink a lot?' asks the doctor.
'Not really, I spill most of it.'

What does the dentist of the year get?
A little plaque.

Two biologists are trying to put radio collars on lions
in the African bush. Before they set off, they pull on
their shoes. One chooses heavy leather hiking boots
and the other a pair of trainers. The man with the hiking
boots says, 'Why are you wearing those?'
The other man replies, 'If the lions get too close
to us we'll have to make a run for it.'
'You're crazy, we'll never outrun a lion,' says the first man.
'That's why I'm wearing the trainers, I only have to outrun you.'

Two explorers are lost in the desert and are desperate for
water. Just as they think they're about to die, they chance
upon a village where market day is in full swing.
They go to the first stall and ask for some water.
'No,' replies the stall owner, 'I only sell fruit.
Try the next stall.'
So off they go to the next stall and again they ask for water.
'Sorry,' says the stall owner, 'I only sell custard.'
The men are now quite desperate and they go to the next
stall, only to be told that the stall only sells jelly.
Hearing this, one man turns to the other and says,
'This is a trifle bazaar!'

A man goes to see his doctor.
'Doctor I have a problem, I can't stop singing
"The Green Green Grass of Home" and "Delilah".
'Sounds as if you have a severe case of
Tom Jones Syndrome,' says the doctor.
'Is it rare?' asks the man.
'No, it's not unusual,' replies the doctor.

**A man went to see his GP and told him
that his arm kept talking to him.
'Don't be ridiculous!' said the doctor.
'No, really,' said the man, 'listen to it.'
So the doctor put his head next to the man's arm
and listened.
'Come on, give us a fiver!' said the arm.
'It's okay,' said the doctor. 'Your arm's broke.'**

A vet goes to see his doctor. The doctor asks the vet
many questions about the symptoms and how long they
have been occurring. The vet is getting increasingly angry,
'Look – I'm a vet. I don't need to ask my patients these kinds
of questions. I can tell what's wrong with them
just by looking. Why can't you?'
The doctor nods and then writes out a prescription.
'There you are. If that doesn't work we'll have
to put you down.'

**Before going to America on business, a man drives his Rolls
Royce into the centre of London and parks it outside a
bank. He asks for an immediate loan of £10,000. The bank
manager asks for collateral and the customer hands over the
keys to his Rolls Royce. The bank manager arranges for the
car to be parked in the bank's underground car park, then
hands over £10,000 in cash. Two weeks later the car owner
returns to the bank and asks to settle his loan.**

'That'll be £10,000 plus £50 interest,' the bank manager tells him. The man immediately writes out a cheque and gives it to the bank manager. As the bank manager is handing over the keys he says, 'While you were away I discovered that you are a millionaire.
Why did you need to borrow the £10,000?'
'Where else could I park my Rolls Royce in the centre of London for £50?' replies the man.

'Do you believe in life after death?' a boss asked one of his employees.
'Yes, Sir.' the new recruit replied.
'Well, then, that makes everything just fine,' the boss went on. 'After you left early yesterday to go to your grandmother's funeral, she stopped in to see you.'

A man's boss came in one morning and caught him hugging his secretary. He said in a rage, 'Is this what you get paid for?' 'No!' the man replied, 'I do this for free.'

A new member of staff was standing in front of the paper shredder with a confused look on her face.
'Do you need any help?' her colleague asked.
'Yeah, how does this thing work?'
The colleague took the papers from her hand and demonstrated how to work the shredder. She stood there a moment with yet another confused expression.
Her colleague said, 'Any questions?'
She said, 'Yeah – exactly where do the copies come out?'

A local business was looking for office help.
They put a sign in the window, stating the following:
'HELP WANTED. Must be able to type, must be good with

a computer and must be bilingual.
We are an Equal Opportunity Employer.'
A short time afterwards, a dog trotted up to the window,
saw the sign and went inside. He looked at the receptionist
and wagged his tail, then walked over to the sign,
looked at it and whined.
Getting the idea, the receptionist got the office manager.
The office manager looked at the dog and was surprised,
to say the least. However, the dog looked determined,
so he led him into the office. Inside, the dog jumped up on
the chair and stared at the manager.
The manager said, 'I can't hire you. The sign says you
have to be able to type.' The dog jumped down, went to
the typewriter and proceeded to type out a perfect letter.
He took out the page and trotted over to the
manager and gave it to him, then
jumped back on the chair.
The manager was stunned, but then
told the dog, 'The sign says you have
to be good with a computer.'
The dog jumped down again and went
to the computer. He proceeded to
enter and execute a perfect
program, which worked
flawlessly the first time.
By this time the manager was
totally dumbfounded!
He looked at the dog and said,
'I realize that you are
a very intelligent dog and have
some interesting abilities.
However, I still can't give you the job.'
The dog jumped down and went to a
copy of the sign and put his paw on
the sentences that told about being an

Equal Opportunity Employer. The manager said, 'Yes, but the sign also says that you have to be bilingual.'
The dog looked at the manager calmly and said, 'Meow!'

A customer sent an order to a distributor for a large amount of goods, totalling a great deal of money.
The distributor noticed that the previous bill hadn't been paid.
The collections manager left a voice-mail for them saying, 'We can't ship your new order until you pay for the last one.'
The next day the collections manager received a collect phone call: 'Please cancel the order. We can't wait that long.'

Caller: I'd like the RSPCA please.
Operator: Where are you calling from?
Caller: The living room.

Caller: The water board please.
Operator: Which department?
Caller: Tap water.

On his deathbed, a businessman phoned his friend and said, 'When I die I want you to make sure I'm cremated.'
'What would you like me to do with your ashes?' asked his friend.
'Send them to the tax man and put a note inside that says, 'Now you have everything'.

A man making heavy breathing sounds from a phone box told the worried operator, 'I haven't got a pen so I'm steaming up the window to write the number on.'

A musical director was having a lot of trouble with one drummer. He talked and talked and talked with the drummer, but his performance simply didn't improve.

Finally, before the whole orchestra, he said, 'When a musician just can't handle his instrument and doesn't improve when given help, they take away the instrument, and give him two sticks, and make him a drummer.'
A stage whisper was heard from the percussion section: 'And if he can't handle even that, they take away one of his sticks and make him a conductor.'

An old blacksmith realized he was soon going to stop working so hard. He picked out a strong young man to become his apprentice. The old fellow was crabby and exacting.
'Don't ask me a lot of questions,' he told the boy.
'Just do whatever I tell you to do.'
One day the old blacksmith took an iron out of the forge and laid it on the anvil. 'Get the hammer over there,' he said.
'When I nod my head, hit it good and hard.'
Now the town is looking for a new blacksmith.

For 30 years, Johnson had arrived at work at 9 a.m. on the dot. He had never missed a day and was never late. Consequently, when on one particular day 9 a.m. passed without Johnson's arrival, it caused a sensation.
All work ceased, and the boss himself, looking at his watch and muttering, came out into the corridor.
Finally, precisely at 10, Johnson showed up, clothes dusty and torn, his face scratched and bruised, his glasses bent. He limped painfully to the time clock, punched in, and said, aware that all eyes were upon him,
'I tripped and rolled down two flights of stairs in the subway. Nearly killed myself.'
And the boss said, 'And to roll down two flights of stairs took you a whole hour?'

Smith goes to see his supervisor in the front office. 'Boss,' he says, 'we're doing some heavy house-cleaning at home

tomorrow, and my wife needs me to help with the attic
and the garage, moving and hauling stuff.'
'We're short-handed, Smith' the boss replies.
'I can't give you the day off.'
'Thanks, boss,' says Smith. 'I knew I could count on you!'

There was a haunted house on the outskirts of
a town that was avoided by all the townsfolk –
all feared the ghost that lived there.
However, an enterprising journalist decided to get the scoop
of the day by photographing the fearsome phantom.
When he entered the house, armed with only his camera,
the ghost descended upon him with his chains clanking.
The journalist told the ghost, 'I mean no harm –
I just want your photograph'. The ghost was quite
happy at this chance to make the headlines, so he
posed for a number of ghostly shots.
The happy journalist rushed back to his darkroom,
and began developing the photos. Unfortunately, they
turned out to be black and underexposed.
So what's the moral of the story?
The spirit was willing but the flash was weak.

A tourist calls a taxi on a dark night. As they drive off,
the passenger taps the driver on the shoulder to ask him
something. The driver screams, loses control of the car, drives
up on to the pavement, and stops inches from a shop window.
The driver says, 'Look friend, don't EVER do that again.
You scared the daylights out of me!'
The passenger apologizes and says he didn't realize
that a 'little tap' could scare him so much. The driver,
after gathering himself replied, 'Sorry, it's not really your fault.
Today is my first day as a taxi driver – I've been driving
hearses for the last twenty-five years!'

Several schoolgirls were beginning to use lipstick and would put it on in the school toilets. That was fine, but after they put on their lipstick they would press their lips to the mirror leaving dozens of little lip prints. Every night, the maintenance man would remove them and the next day, the girls would put them back. Finally the head teacher decided that something had to be done.

She called all the girls to the toilets and met them there with the maintenance man. She explained that all these lip prints were causing a major problem for the man who had to clean the mirrors every night. To demonstrate how difficult it had been to clean the mirrors, she asked the maintenance man to show the girls how much effort was required.

He took out a long-handled squeegee mop, dipped it in the toilet, and cleaned the mirror with it.

Since then, there have been no lip prints on the mirror.

A customer goes into a restaurant and as he does so he notices a sign, saying '$150 if we fail to provide your order'.
When his waitress arrives he orders elephant dung on rye.
She calmly writes the order down and walks into the kitchen.
The restaurant owner comes storming out,
lays $150 on the man's table and says, 'You got us this time!
It's been years since we've run out of rye bread.'

The assistant in the chemist could never find what the customers wanted. He had been warned that the next sale missed would be his last.

A man came into the shop coughing and when he asked the assistant for some cough medicine, the assistant couldn't find it anywhere. Rather than alert the boss to the problem he substituted Ex-Lax for the cough mixture and told the man to take it all at once.

When his boss came over, the assistant explained what he had done.

'Ex-Lax won't cure a cough!' shouted the boss.
'Yes it will,' said the boy, 'he won't dare to cough.'

'I've got good news and bad news,' says the
policeman to the suspect.
'What's the bad news?' asks the suspect.
'Your blood matches the DNA that we found at the murder
scene,' replies the policeman.
'Oh no,' replies the suspect. 'What's the good news?'
'You've got very low cholesterol.'

A man hosted a dinner party for people from work,
including his boss. Throughout the meal, the host's three-
year-old daughter stared at her father's boss, who was sitting
opposite her. The girl could hardly eat her food for staring.
The man checked his tie, felt his face for food, patted his
hair in place, but nothing stopped her from staring at him.
He tried his best to just ignore her
but finally it was too much for him.
He asked her, 'Why are you staring at me?'
The little girl replied, 'My Daddy said you drink
like a fish and I don't want to miss it!'

A large lumberjack company were advertising for a good
lumberjack. Soon after the advertisement was posted,
a skinny man arrived at the door with his axe.
'You're not built for lumberjacking,' said the owner.
'Just give me a chance and I'll prove to you what I can do,'
replied the skinny man.
'Okay,' said the boss. 'You see that giant tree over there,
take your axe and cut it down.'
Five minutes later the skinny man was back, claiming he had
felled the tree. The boss couldn't believe his eyes when he
looked out of the window.

'Where did you learn to chop down trees like that?' he asked.
'In the Sahara Forest,' replied the skinny man.
'You mean the Sahara Desert,' said the boss.
'Yes, that's what they call it now.'

**A shoplifter was caught red-handed trying to steal a watch
from an exclusive jewellery shop.
'Listen,' he said, 'I know you don't want any trouble.
'What do you say I just buy the watch and we forget about it?'
The manager agreed and wrote up the sales slip.
The crook looked at the slip and said, 'This is a little more
than I intended to spend.
Can you show me something less expensive?'**

The teacher asked the children to each bring an electrical
appliance to class. Wendy took a personal stereo and
explained you could play music on it. Stuart took an electrical
tin opener and explained how it worked. When it was
Johnnie's turn, he told the class his item was
outside in the hall, so they all went out to have a look.
'It's a heart and lung machine, Miss. They use it in the
hospital to keep your heart going.'
'What did your father say about bringing this to school Johnnie?'
'Not much miss. He just said "Aaaaargh".'

**An man was filling out a job application.
When he came to the question, 'Have you
ever been arrested?' he answered, 'No'.
The next question, intended for people who had answered in
the affirmative to the last one, was 'Why?' The applicant
answered it anyway: 'Never got caught.'**

Did you hear about the new restaurant on the Moon?
Great food but no atmosphere.

Two lawyers went into a restaurant and ordered two drinks. Then they produced sandwiches from their briefcases and started to eat. The waiter marched over and told them, 'You can't eat your own sandwiches in here!' The attorneys looked at each other, shrugged their shoulders and then exchanged sandwiches.

An applicant was being interviewed for admission to a prominent medical school. 'Tell me,' inquired the interviewer, 'where do you expect to be ten years from now?' 'Well, let's see,' replied the student. 'It's Wednesday afternoon. I guess I'll be on the golf course by now.'

'In this job we need someone who is responsible.' 'I'm the one you want. On my last job, every time anything went wrong, they said I was responsible.'

'Young man, do you think you can handle a variety of work?' 'I ought to be able to. I've had ten different jobs in four months.'

A navy psychiatrist was interviewing a potential sailor. To check on the young man's response to trouble, the psychiatrist asked, 'What would you do if you looked out of that window right now and saw a battleship.' The young sailor said, 'I'd grab a torpedo and sink it.' 'Where would you get the torpedo?' 'The same place you got your battleship!'

Several weeks after a young man had been hired,
he was called into the personnel manager's office.
'What is the meaning of this?' the manager asked. 'When you
applied for the job, you told us you had five years' experience.
Now we discover this is the first job you've ever had.'
'Well,' the young man said, 'in your ad you said you wanted
somebody with imagination.'

**'Why are you so excited?' the surgeon asked the patient that
was about to be anaesthetised.
'But doctor, this is my first operation.'
'Really? It's mine too, and I'm not excited at all.'**

A young man, hired by a supermarket, reported for his
first day of work. The manager greeted him with a warm
handshake and a smile, gave him a broom and said,
'Your first job will be to sweep out the store.'
'But I'm a college graduate,' the young man replied.
'Oh, I'm sorry. I didn't know that,' said the manager.
'Here, give me the broom, I'll show you how.'

**The manager of a clothing shop is reviewing a potential
employee's application and notices that the man has never
worked in retail before. He says to the man, 'For a man with
no experience, you are certainly asking for a high wage.'
'Well Sir,' the applicant replies, 'the work is so much harder
when you don't know what you're doing!'**

Two women were comparing notes on the difficulties
of running a small business. 'I started a new practice last year,'
the first one said. 'I insist that each of my employees takes at
least a week off every three months.'
'Why in the world would you do that?' the other asked.
She responded, 'It's the best way I know of to learn
which ones I can do without.'

A man stopped at a petrol station and, after filling his tank, he bought a soft drink. He stood by his car to drink and watched a couple of men working along the roadside. One man would dig a hole two or three feet deep and then move on. The other man came along behind and filled in the hole. While one was digging a new hole, the other was about 25 feet behind filling in the old.

'Hold it, hold it,' the fellow said to the men. 'Can you tell me what's going on here with this digging?'

'Well, we work for the city council,' one of the men said.

'But one of you is digging a hole and the other is filling it up. You're not accomplishing anything. Aren't you wasting the tax-payer's money?'

'You don't understand, mister,' one of the men said, leaning on his shovel and wiping his brow. 'Normally there's three of us, me, Joe and Mike. I dig the hole, Joe sticks in the tree and Mike here puts the dirt back.'

'Yeah,' piped up Mike. 'Now just because Joe is sick, that doesn't mean we can't work, does it?'

Negotiations between union members and their employer were at an impasse. The union denied that their workers were flagrantly abusing their contract's sick-leave provisions. One morning at the bargaining table, the company's chief negotiator held aloft the morning edition of the newspaper. 'This man,' he announced, 'called in sick yesterday!' There, on the sports page, was a photo of the supposedly ill employee, who had just won a local golf tournament with an excellent score. A union negotiator broke the silence in the room. 'Wow,' he said. 'Think of what kind of score he could have had if he hadn't been sick!'

The manager of a large office noticed a new man one day and told him to come into his office. 'What is your name?'

was the first thing the manager asked him.

'John,' the new man replied.

The manager scowled, 'Look, I don't know what kind of a place you worked at before, but I don't call anyone by their first name. It breeds familiarity and that leads to a breakdown in authority. I refer to my employees by their last name only – Smith, Jones, Baker – that's all. I am to be referred to only as Mr Thompson. Now that we got that straight, what is your last name?'

The new man sighed and said,

'Darling. My name is John Darling.'

'Okay, John, the next thing I want to tell you is...'

'I have to have a raise,' the man said to his boss.

'There are three other companies after me.'

'Is that so?' asked the manager.

'What other companies are after you?'

'The electric company, the telephone company, and the gas company.'

A nurse walked into the maternity waiting room and said to one man, 'Congratulations sir, you're the new father of twins!'

The man replied, 'How about that, I work for the Doublemint Chewing Gum Company!'

About an hour later, the same nurse entered the waiting room and announced that another man had just had triplets.

'Well, how do you like that,' he said.

'I work for the 3M Company.'

A third man then got up and started to leave, saying,

'I think I need a breath of fresh air – I work for 7-UP'.

Two social workers were walking through a rough part of the city in the evening. They heard moans and muted cries for help from a back lane. Upon investigation, they found a semi-conscious man in a pool of blood.

'Help me, I've been mugged and viciously beaten,' he pleaded.
The two social workers turned and walked away.
One remarked to her colleague,
'You know the person that did this really needs help.'

A man has a heart attack and is taken to the hospital
emergency department. The doctor tells him that he will not
live unless he has a heart transplant right away.
Another doctor runs into the room and says,
'You're in luck, two hearts just became available, and so you
will get to choose which one you want. One belongs to a
lawyer and the other to a social worker.'
The man quickly responds, 'The lawyer's'.
The doctor says, 'Wait! Don't you want to know a little
about them before you make your decision?'
The man says, 'I already know enough. We all know that
social workers are bleeding hearts and the lawyer's probably
never used his, so I'll take the lawyer's!'

A doctor and his wife were having a big argument
at breakfast.'You aren't so good in bed either!'
he shouted, and stormed off to work.
By mid-morning, he decided he'd better make amends and
phoned home. After many rings, his wife picked up the phone.
'What took you so long to answer?'
'I was in bed.'
'What were you doing in bed this late?'
'Getting a second opinion.'

A man goes to his doctor for a complete check up.
He hasn't been feeling well and wants to find out if he's ill.
After the check up the doctor comes out
with the results of the examination.
'I'm afraid I have some bad news. You're dying and you

don't have much time,' the doctor says.
'Oh no, that's terrible. How long have I got?' the man asks.
'Ten...' says the doctor.
'Ten? Ten what? Months? Weeks? What?' he asks.
'Nine ... eight ... seven ...'

A young woman went to her doctor complaining of pain.
'Where are you hurting?' asked the doctor.
'You have to help me, I hurt all over', said the woman.
'What do you mean, all over?' asked the doctor.
'Be a little more specific.'
The woman touched her right knee with her index finger and
yelled, 'Ow, that hurts.' Then she touched her left cheek and
again yelled, 'Ouch! That hurts, too.' Then she touched her
right earlobe, 'Ow, even that hurts,' she cried.
The doctor checked her thoughtfully for a moment and told
her his diagnosis. 'You have a broken finger.'

**'Doctor, are you sure I'm suffering from pneumonia?
I've heard about a doctor treating someone with
pneumonia and finally he died of typhus.'
'Don't worry, it won't happen to me. If I treat someone with
pneumonia he will die of pneumonia.'**

A man went to see his doctor because he was suffering from a
miserable cold. His doctor prescribed some pills,
but they didn't help. On his next visit the doctor gave
him an injection, but that didn't do any good either.
On his third visit the doctor told the man, 'Go home and take
a hot bath. As soon as you finish bathing throw
open all the windows and stand in the draft.'
'But doctor,' protested the patient,
'if I do that, I'll get pneumonia.'
'I know,' said the doctor. 'I can cure pneumonia.'

A pipe burst in a doctor's house. He called a plumber.
The plumber arrived, unpacked his tools, did mysterious
plumber-type things for a while, and handed the doctor a
huge bill. The doctor exclaimed, 'This is ridiculous!
I don't even make that much as a doctor!' The plumber
quietly answered, 'Neither did I when I was a doctor.'

'The doctor said he would have me on my feet in two weeks.'
'And did he?'
'Yes, I had to sell the car to pay the bill.'

A man walked into a doctor's and the receptionist asked him
what he had. He said, 'Shingles'.
So she took down his name, address, his national insurance
number and told him to have a seat.
A few minutes later a nurse came out and asked him what
he had. He said, 'Shingles'.
So she took down his height, weight, his complete medical
history and told him to wait in the examining room.
Ten minutes later another nurse came in and asked him
what he had. He said, 'Shingles'.
So she gave him a blood test, a blood-pressure test,
an electrocardiogram, told him to take off all his clothes
and wait for the doctor.
Fifteen minutes later the doctor came in and asked
him what he had. He said, 'Shingles'.
The doctor said, 'Where?'
He said, 'Outside in the truck. Where do you want them?'

A woman, calling the local hospital, said,
'Hello, I want to know if a patient is getting better.'
The voice on the other end of the line said, 'What is the
patient's name and room number?'
She said, 'Sarah Brown, in Room 311'.

He said, 'Oh, yes. Mrs Brown is doing very well.
In fact, she's had two full meals, her blood pressure is fine,
she's going to be taken off the heart monitor in a couple of
hours and if she continues this improvement, Dr Phillips is
going to send her home on Tuesday.'
The woman said, 'Thank God! That's wonderful! Oh!
That's fantastic! That's wonderful news!'
The man on the phone said, 'From your enthusiasm,
I take it you must be a close family member or
a very close friend!'
She said, 'I'm Sarah Brown in 311!
My doctor doesn't tell me a thing!'

**A man goes to the optician. The receptionist asks him
why he is there. The man complains, 'I keep seeing spots
in front of my eyes.'
The receptionist asks,
'Have you ever seen a doctor?'
and the man replies, 'No, just spots.'**

Patient: 'I always see spots before my eyes.'
Doctor: 'Didn't the new glasses help?'
Patient: 'Sure, now I see the spots
much clearer.'

**A doctor tells a man needing a heart
insplant that the only heart available is that of
sheep. The man finally agrees and the doctor
insplants the sheep heart into the man. A few
?ks after the operation, the man comes in for a
check up. The doctor asks him,
'How are you feeling?'
The man replies 'Not BAAAAD!'**

Dentist: 'I have to pull the aching tooth,
but don't worry it will take just five minutes.'
Patient: 'And how much will it cost?'
Dentist: 'It's £90.00.'
Patient: '£90.00 for just a few minutes work?'
Dentist: 'I can extract it very slowly if you like.'

**'I came in to make an appointment with the dentist,'
said the man to the receptionist.
'I'm sorry sir.' she replied. 'He's out right now, but ...'
'Thank you,' interrupted the obviously nervous prospective
patient. 'When will he be out again?'**

A husband and wife entered the dentist's office. The husband
said, 'I want a tooth pulled. I don't want gas or a pain killer
because I'm in a terrible hurry.
Just pull the tooth as quickly as possible.'
'You're a brave man,' said the dentist. 'Now, show me which
tooth it is.'
The husband turns to his wife and says, 'Open your mouth and
show the dentist which tooth it is, dear.'

**A doctor is going round the ward with a nurse and they
come to the first bed where the patient looks very ill.
'Did you give this man two tablets every eight hours?'
asks the doctor.
'Oh, no,' replies the nurse, 'I gave him eight tablets
every two hours!'
At the next bed the next patient also appears distressed.
'Nurse, did you give this man one tablet every twelve hours?'
'Oops, I gave him twelve tablets every one hour,'
replies the nurse.
Unfortunately at the next bed the patient has died.
'Nurse,' asks the doctor, 'did you prick his boil?'**

A biologist phones his wife from his office and says, 'Honey,
something has just come up, I realize it's the weekend, but I
have to visit my field site for a few days. So, would you pack
my clothes, my field equipment and my blue silk pyjamas?
I'll be home in an hour to pick them up.'
A week later he returned. 'Did you have a good trip, dear?'
his wife asked.
'Oh, it was just a typical field trip, you know,work work work,'
he exclaimed, and added 'But you forgot to pack
my blue silk pyjamas.'
'No I didn't,' she replied. 'I put them in the box of equipment!'

**A teacher set a schoolboy an essay to write on childbirth,
and the boy asked his mother, 'How was I born?'
'Well dear,' said the slightly prudish mother,
'the stork brought you to us.'
'Oh,' said the boy, 'and how did you and Daddy get born?'
'Oh, the stork brought us too.'
'Well how were Grandpa and Grandma born?'
the boy persisted.
'Well darling, the stork brought them too!' said the mother.
Several days later, the boy handed in his essay to the teacher
who read with confusion the opening sentence:
'This report has been very difficult to write due to the fact
that there hasn't been a natural childbirth in my family for
three generations.'**

One day, a zookeeper noticed that the orang-utan was reading
two books – the Bible and Darwin's *Origin of the Species*.
In surprise he asked the ape,
'Why are you reading both those books'?
'Well,' said the orang-utan, 'I just wanted to know if I was my
brother's keeper or my keeper's brother.'

A biologist was interested in studying how far bullfrogs can jump. He brought a bullfrog into his laboratory, set it down, and commanded, 'Jump, frog, jump!'
The frog jumped across the room.
The biologist measured the distance, then noted in his journal, 'Frog with four legs jumped eight feet.'
Then he cut the frog's front legs off. Again he ordered, 'Jump, frog, jump!'
The frog struggled a moment, then jumped a few feet.
After measuring the distance, the biologist noted in his journal, 'Frog with two legs jumped three feet.'
Next, the biologist cut off the frog's back legs. Once more, he shouted, 'Jump, frog, jump!' The frog just lay there.
'Jump, frog, jump!' the biologist repeated. Nothing.
The biologist noted in his journal, 'Frog with no legs – lost its hearing.'

An elderly woman went into the doctor's office. When the doctor asked why she was there, she replied, 'I'd like to have some birth control pills.'
Taken aback, the doctor thought for a minute and then said, 'Excuse me, Mrs Smith, but you're 75 years old.
What possible use could you have for birth control pills?'
The woman responded, 'They help me sleep better'.
The doctor thought some more and continued,
'How in the world do birth control pills help you to sleep?'
The woman said, 'I put them in my granddaughter's orange juice and I sleep better at night'.

A chemist looks out the front of the shop and sees a woman holding a bottle jumping up and down in the parking lot.
The chemist walks out to the parking lot and asks the woman what's the matter. She replies 'I saw it said "Shake Well" after I took it'.

A funeral procession is going up a steep hill on a main road when the door of the hearse flies open and the coffin falls out and crashes into a chemist shop. The lid pops open and the deceased says to the astonished assistant,
'You got anything to stop this coffin?'

A lawyer's son wanted to follow in his father's footsteps, so he went to law school. He graduated with honours, and then went home to join his father's firm. At the end of his first day at work he rushed into his father's office, and said,
'Father, father, in one day I have solved the accident case that you've been working on for ten years!'
His father responded, 'You idiot, we could have lived off that case for another ten years!'

A lawyer opened the door of his BMW, and suddenly a car came along and hit the door, ripping it off completely. When the police arrived at the scene, the lawyer was complaining bitterly about the damage to his precious BMW.
'Officer, look what they've done to my car!' he whined.
'You lawyers are so materialistic,' retorted the officer.
'You're so worried about your BMW, that you didn't even notice that your left arm has been ripped off!'
'Oh my God!' replied the lawyer. 'Where's my Rolex?'

A woman and her little girl were visiting the grave of the little girl's grandmother. On their way through the cemetery back to the car, the little girl asked,
'Mummy, do they ever bury two people in the same grave?'
'Of course not, dear,' replied the mother,
'Why would you think that?'
'The gravestone back there said,
"Here lies a lawyer and an honest man".'

A group of terrorists hijacked a plane full of lawyers.
They called down to ground control with their list of demands
and added that if these weren't met, they would release one
lawyer every hour.

**A red-faced judge convened court after a
long lunch.
The first case involved a man charged
with drunk driving, who claimed it simply
wasn't true.
'I'm as sober as you are, your honour,'
the man claimed.
The judge replied, 'Clerk, please
enter a guilty plea.
The defendant is sentenced to
thirty days.'**

The judge asked the defendant, 'Mr
Jones, do you understand that you have
sworn to tell the truth, the whole truth
and nothing but the truth?'
'I do.'
'Now what do you say to defend yourself?'
'Under those limitations ... nothing.'

**'Doctor, how many autopsies have you performed
on dead people?'
'All my autopsies are on dead people.'**

An accountant visited the Natural History museum.
While standing near the dinosaur he said to his neighbour,
'This dinosaur is two billion years and ten months old'.
'Where did you get this exact information?'
'I was here ten months ago, and the guide told me that the
dinosaur is two billion years old.'

The defendant stood up in the dock and said to the judge,
'I don't recognize this court!'
'Why?' asked the judge
'Because you've had it decorated since the
last time I was here.'

Two accountants are in a bank when armed robbers burst in.
While several of the robbers take the money from the tellers,
others line the customers, including the accountants, up
against a wall, and proceed to take their wallets, watches, etc.
While this is going on accountant number one jams something
in accountant number two's hand. Without looking down,
accountant number two whispers, 'What is this?' to which
accountant number one replies, 'it's that £50 I owe you.'

**An accountant is having a hard time sleeping and goes to
see his doctor. 'Doctor, I just can't get to sleep at night.'
'Have you tried counting sheep?'
'That's the problem – I make a mistake and then spend
three hours trying to find it.'**

A patient was at her doctor's office after undergoing a
complete physical exam. The doctor said, 'I have some very
grave news for you. You only have six months to live.'
The patient asked, 'Oh doctor, what should I do?'
The doctor replied, 'Marry an accountant'.
'Will that make me live longer?' asked the patient.
'No,' said the doctor, 'but it will SEEM longer.'

A man in a bar leans over to the man next to him and says,
'Want to hear an accountant joke?'
The man next to him replies, 'Well, before you tell that
joke, you should know that I'm six feet tall, 200 pounds, and
I'm an accountant. And the man sitting next to me is six
feet two inches tall, 225 pounds, and he's an accountant.

Now, do you still want to tell that joke?'
'No, I don't want to have to explain it twice.'

If an accountant's wife cannot sleep, what does she say?
'Darling, could you tell me about your work.'

**A business owner tells her friend that she is
desperately searching for an accountant.
Her friend asks, 'Didn't your company hire an accountant
a short while ago?' The business owner replies,
'That's the accountant I've been searching for.'**

A young accountant spends a week at his new office with the
retiring accountant he is replacing. Each and every morning as
the more experienced accountant begins the day, he opens his
desk drawer, takes out a worn envelope, removes a yellowing
sheet of paper, reads it, nods his head, looks around the room
with renewed vigour, returns the envelope to the drawer,
and then begins his day's work.
After he retires, the new accountant can hardly wait to read
for himself the message contained in the envelope in the
drawer, particularly since he feels so inadequate in replacing
the far wiser and more highly esteemed accountant.
Surely, he thinks to himself, it must contain the great secret to
his success, a wondrous treasure of inspiration and motivation.
His fingers tremble anxiously as he removes the mysterious
envelope from the drawer and reads the following message:
'Debits in the column towards the filing cabinet.
Credits in the column towards the window.'

**The difference between the short and long income-tax forms
is simple. If you use the short form, the government gets
your money. If you use the long form, the tax advisor gets
your money.**

Why won't sharks attack tax inspectors?
Professional courtesy.

'How have you managed to buy such a luxurious villa while
your income is so low?' asked the tax inspector.
'Well,' the taxpayer answered, 'while fishing last summer I
caught a large golden fish. When I took it off the hook, the
fish opened his mouth and said, "I am a magical fish. Throw
me back to the sea and I'll give you the most luxurious villa
you have ever seen."
I threw the fish back to the sea, and got the villa.'
'How can you prove such an unbelievable story?'
'Well, you can see the villa, can't you?'

A nervous taxpayer was unhappily conversing with the tax
inspector who had come to review his records. At one point the
tax inspector exclaimed, 'We feel it is a great privilege to be
allowed to live and work in this country.
As a citizen you have an obligation to pay taxes,
and we expect you to eagerly pay them with a smile.'
'Thank God,' returned the taxpayer.
'I thought you were going to want cash.'

A man, about to enter hospital, saw two white-coated
doctors searching through the flowerbeds.
'Excuse me,' he said, 'have you lost something?'
'No,' replied one of the doctors. 'We're doing
a heart transplant for an income-tax inspector
and want to find a suitable stone.'

A fine is a tax for doing something wrong.
A tax is a fine for doing something right.

Three men are fishing in the Caribbean.
The first man says, 'I had a terrible fire; lost everything.

Now the insurance company is paying for everything and that's why I'm here.'

The second man says, 'I had a terrible explosion; lost everything. Now the insurance company is paying for everything and that's why I'm here.'

The third man says, 'What a coincidence. I had a terrible flood; lost everything. Now the insurance company is paying for everything and that's why I'm here.'

The other two men turned to him with confusion and asked, 'Flood? How do you start a flood?'

'You ought to feel highly honoured,' said the businessman to the life-insurance agent. 'So far today I have had my secretary turn away seven insurance agents.'

'Yes, I know,' replied the agent. 'I'm them.'

A salesman was demonstrating unbreakable combs in a department store, impressing the people who stopped to look by putting the comb through all sorts of torture and stress.

Finally, to impress even the sceptics in the crowd, he bent the comb completely in half, and it snapped with a loud crack. Without pausing, he bravely held up both halves of the 'unbreakable' comb for everyone to see and said, 'And this, ladies and gentlemen, is what an unbreakable comb looks like on the inside.'

Two shoe salespeople were sent to Africa to open up new markets. Three days after arriving, one salesperson called the office and said, 'I'm returning on the next flight. Can't sell shoes here. Everybody goes barefoot.'

At the same time the other salesperson sent an email to the factory stating, 'The prospects are unlimited. Nobody wears shoes here!'

A door-to-door vacuum-cleaner salesman manages to convince a woman in the depths of the countryside to let him into her house. 'This machine is the best ever,' he exclaims, whilst pouring a bag of dirt over the lounge floor. The woman says she's really worried it may not all come off, so the salesman says, 'If this machine doesn't remove all the dust completely, I'll lick it off myself.'
'Do you want ketchup on it?' she says.
'We're not connected for electricity yet!'

A golfer, practising alone, is about to tee off, when a salesman runs up to him and yells, 'Wait! Before you tee off, I have something really amazing to show you!'
The golfer, annoyed, says, 'What is it?'
'It's a special golf ball,' says the salesman. 'You can never lose it!'
'What do you mean,' scoffs the golfer, 'you can never lose it? What if you hit it into the water?'
'No problem,' says the salesman. 'It floats, and it detects where the shore is, and spins towards it.'
'Well, what if you hit it into the woods?'
'Easy,' says the salesman. 'It emits a beeping sound, and you can find it with your eyes closed.'
'Okay,' says the golfer, impressed. 'But what if your round goes late and it gets dark?'
'No problem, sir, this golf ball glows in the dark! I'm telling you, you can never lose this golf ball!'
The golfer puts his hand in his pocket, ready to buy one. 'Just one question,' he says to the salesman. 'Where did you get it?'
'I found it.'

A sales manager and an operations manager went bear hunting. While the operations manager stayed in the cabin, the sales manager went out looking for a bear.
He soon found a huge bear, shot at it, but only wounded it.

The enraged bear charged toward the sales manager,
who started running for the cabin as fast as he could.
He ran pretty fast but the bear was just a little faster
and gained on him with every step.
Just as he reached the open cabin door, he tripped and
fell flat. Too close behind to stop, the bear jumped
over him and went rolling into the cabin.
The sales manager jumped up, closed the cabin door and
yelled to his friend inside, 'You skin this one
while I go and get another!'

A man went into a bookshop and asked the saleswoman,
'Where's the self-help section?'
She answered, 'If I tell you, it will defeat the purpose.'

A young banker decided to get his first tailor-made suit.
So he went to the finest tailor in town and got measured.
A week later he went in for his first fitting.
He put on the suit and he looked stunning,
he felt that in this suit he could do business.
As he was preening himself in front of the mirror he
reached down to put his hands in the pockets and to his
surprise he noticed that there were none.
He mentioned this to the tailor who asked him,
'Didn't you tell me you were a banker?'
The young man answered, 'Yes, I did'.
To this the tailor said, 'Who ever heard of a banker
with his hands in his own pockets?'

A film crew was on location deep in the desert. One day an old
Indian went up to the director and said, 'Tomorrow rain.'
The next day it rained. A week later, the Indian went up to
the director and said, 'Tomorrow storm.'
The next day there was a hailstorm.

'This Indian is incredible,' said the director. He told his secretary to hire the Indian to predict the weather. However, after several successful predictions, the old Indian didn't show up for two weeks. Finally the director sent for him. 'I have to shoot a big scene tomorrow,' said the director, 'and I'm depending on you. What will the weather be like?'
The Indian shrugged his shoulders. 'Don't know,' he said.
'Radio is broken.'

A newsboy was standing on the corner with a stack of papers, yelling, 'Read all about it. Fifty people swindled! Fifty people swindled!'
Curious, a man walked over, bought a paper, and checked the front page. Finding nothing, the man said, 'There's nothing in here about fifty people being swindled.'
The newsboy ignored him and went on, calling out, 'Read all about it. Fifty-one people swindled!'

At a country-club party a young man was introduced to an attractive girl. Immediately he began paying her court and flattering her outrageously. The girl liked the young man, but his fast and ardent pitch took her a bit aback. She was amazed when after 30 minutes he seriously proposed marriage.
'Look,' she said. 'We only met a half hour ago. How can you be so sure? We know nothing about each other.'
'You're wrong,' the young man declared.
'For the past five years I've been working in the bank where your father has his account.'

A photographer for a national newspaper was assigned the task of getting photos of a great forest fire. Smoke at the scene was too thick to get any good shots, so he frantically called his home office to hire a plane.
'It will be waiting for you at the airport!' he was assured by his editor. As soon as he got to the small, rural airport,

sure enough, a plane was warming up near the runway.

He jumped in with his equipment and yelled, 'Let's go! Let's go!' The pilot swung the plane into the wind and soon they were in the air.

'Fly over the north side of the fire,' said the photographer, 'and make three or four low-level passes.'

'Why?' asked the pilot.

'Because I'm going to take pictures! I'm a photographer, and photographers take pictures!' said the photographer with great exasperation.

After a long pause the pilot said, 'You mean you're not the instructor?'

The Walton's invited their new neighbours over to dinner. During dinner, Mr Walton was asked what he did for a living. Eight-year-old Brian Walton jumped in and said, 'Daddy is a fisherman!' To which Mrs Walton replied, 'Brian, why do say that? Your daddy is a stockbroker, not a fisherman.'

'No Mum. Every time we visit Dad at work and he hangs up the phone, he laughs, rubs his hands together and says "I just caught another fish".'

How can you tell that there's a drummer at your front door? The knocking gets faster and faster.

How can you tell that there's a vocalist at your front door?
She forgets the key and doesn't know when to come in.

A couple were having marital difficulties and consulted a
marriage counsellor. During the meeting, the counsellor told
them that their problems could all be traced to a lack of
communication. 'You two need to talk,' he said.
'So, I recommend that you go to a jazz club.
Just wait until it's time for the bass player's solo
and you'll be talking just like everyone else.'

What's the definition of a gentleman?
Someone that can play the bagpipes but doesn't.

The doorbell rang and the lady of the house discovered
a workman, complete with tool chest, on the front porch.
'Madam,' he announced, 'I'm the piano tuner.'
The lady exclaimed, 'Why, I didn't send for a piano tuner.'
The man replied, 'I know you didn't,
but your neighbours did.'

An artist asked the gallery owner if there had been
any interest in his paintings on display at that time.
'I have good news and bad news,' the owner replied.
'The good news is that a gentleman enquired about your work
and wondered if it would appreciate in value after your death.
When I told him it would, he bought all fifteen of your paintings.'
'That's wonderful,' the artist exclaimed. 'What's the bad news?'
'He was your doctor...'

An artist had been working on a nude portrait for a long
time. Every day, he was up early and worked late – bringing
perfection with every stroke of his paintbrush. As each day
passed, he gained a better understanding of the female body
and was able to really make his paintings shine.

After a month, the artist had become very weary from this non-stop effort and decided to take it easy for the day. Since his model had already shown up, he suggested they merely have a glass of wine and talk, since normally he preferred to do his painting in silence.
They talked for a few hours, getting to know each other better. Then as they were sipping their wine, the artist heard a car arriving outside. He jumped up and said, 'Oh no! It's my wife! Quick, take off your clothes!'

Artist Pablo Picasso surprised a burglar at work in his new chateau. The intruder got away, but Picasso told the police he could do a rough sketch of what he looked like. On the basis of his drawing, the police arrested a mother superior, the minister of finance, a washing machine and the Eiffel Tower.

A little girl came home from school and said to her mother, 'Mummy, today in school I was punished for something that I didn't do.'
The mother exclaimed, 'But that's terrible! I'm going to have a talk with your teacher about this.
What was it that you didn't do?'
The little girl replied, 'My homework'.

A teacher was having trouble teaching arithmetic to one little boy. So she said, 'If you reached in your right pocket and found a penny, and you reached in your left pocket and found another one, what would you have?'
'Somebody else's pants.'

A biology teacher said to his class, 'Now I'll show you this frog in my pocket'. He reached into his pocket and pulled out a chicken sandwich. He looked puzzled for a second, and said, 'That's odd. I distinctly remember eating my lunch.'

'Haven't I seen your face before?' a judge demanded, looking
down at the defendant.
'You have, Your Honour,' the man answered hopefully.
'I gave your son violin lessons last winter.'
'Ah, yes,' recalled the judge. 'Twenty years!'

**It was mealtime on a small airline and a flight attendant
asked a passenger if he would like dinner.
'What are my choices?' he asked.
'Yes or No,' she replied.**

After the first takeoff of the fully automatic plane,
the passengers heard the soothing, reassuring voice
of the pilot: 'Ladies and gentlemen, this is your automatic
pilot. In my modern and carefully tested system an error is
absolutely impossible, absolutely impossible,
absolutely impossible...'

**Taxiing down the runway, a plane abruptly stopped,
turned around and returned to the gate. After an hour-long
wait, it finally took off. A concerned passenger asked
the flight attendant, 'What was the problem?'
'The pilot was bothered by a noise he heard in the engine,'
explained the flight attendant,
'and it took us a while to find a new pilot.'**

A kangaroo kept getting out of his enclosure at the zoo.
Knowing that he could hop high, the zoo officials put up
a 10-foot fence. He was out the next morning,
just roaming around the zoo. A 20-foot fence was put up.
Again he got out. When the fence was 40 feet high,
a camel in the next enclosure asked the kangaroo,
'How high do you think they'll go?'
The kangaroo said, 'About a thousand feet, unless somebody
locks the gate at night!'

An unemployed man got a new job at the zoo. He was told
to dress up in a gorilla's skin and pretend to be a gorilla so
people would keep coming to the zoo.
On his first day on the job, the man puts on the skin and
went into the cage. The people all cheered to see him.
He started really putting on a show, jumping around,
beating his chest and roaring.
During one acrobatic attempt, he lost his balance and
crashed through some safety netting, landing squarerly in
the middle of the lion cage! As he lay there stunned, the
lion roared. The man was terrified and started screaming,
'Help! Help!'
The lion raced over to him, placed his paws on his chest and
hissed, 'Shut up or we'll both lose our jobs!'

A man went to work for a zoo vet.
'Look in the lion's mouth,' the vet told him.
'How do I do that?' he asked.
'Carefully,' replied the vet.

A person checks into a hotel for the first time in his life, and
goes up to his room. Five minutes later he calls the desk and
says, 'You've given me a room with no exit. How do I leave?'
The desk clerk says, 'Have you looked for the door?'
The person says, ' Well, there's one door that leads to the
bathroom. There's a second door that goes into the
cupboard. And there's a door I haven't tried,
but it has a "do not disturb" sign on it.'

A man walks into a bar and orders a beer. While chatting with
the barman, the man says, 'I have a method that will enable
you to double the amount of beer you sell every day.'
'Really?' says the bartender, 'How?'
'Very simple, just pour full glasses.'

A man went into a bar and ordered a martini. Before drinking it, he removed the olive and carefully put it into a glass jar. Then he ordered another martini and did the same thing. After an hour, when he was full of martinis and the jar was full of olives, he staggered out.
'Well,' said a customer, 'I never saw anything as peculiar as that!'
'What's so peculiar about it?' the barman said. 'His wife probably sent him out for a jar of olives.'

A man rushes into a bar, orders four expensive 30-year-old single malt whiskies and has the barman line them up in front of him. Without pausing, he quickly drinks each one.
'Whew,' the barman remarked, 'you seem to be in a hurry.'
'You would be too if you had what I have.'
'What do you have?' the bartender sympathetically asked.
'Fifty pence.'

A man walks into a bar and asks the barman to recommend a good drink. The barman says that their 'grasshoppers' are very good, so the man orders one.
Then he has another couple.
On the way home he notices a grasshopper on the ground.
He says to the grasshopper, 'do you know that there is a drink named after you?'
The grasshopper looks up at the man and says, 'They have a drink called Kevin?'

A Post Office worker at the main sorting office finds an unstamped, poorly hand-written envelope addressed to God. He opens it and discovers it is from an elderly lady, distressed because some thief has robbed her of £100. She will be cold and hungry for the rest of the month if she doesn't receive some divine intervention.

The worker organizes a collection amongst the other postal workers, who dig deep and come up with £96.
They get it to her by special courier the same morning.
A week later, the same postal worker recognizes the same handwriting on another envelope. He opens it and reads:
'Dear God, Thank you for the £100. This month would have been so bleak otherwise. P.S. It was four pounds short but that was probably those thieving lot at the Post Office.'

A woman went to the Post Office to buy stamps for her Christmas Cards. 'What denomination?' asked the assistant. 'Oh, good heavens! Have we come to this?' said the woman. 'Well, give me thirty Catholic, ten Baptist ones, twenty Latter Day Saints and forty Mormon.'

A farmer, who went to a big city to see the sights, asked the hotel's clerk about the time of meals.
'Breakfast is served from 7 to 11, dinner from 12 to 3, and supper from 6 to 8,' explained the clerk.
'Look here,' inquired the farmer in surprise, 'when am I going to get time to see the city?'

A police officer pulls over a man who had been weaving in and out of the lanes of traffic. He goes up to the man's window and says, 'Sir, I need you to blow into this

breathalyzer tube.'
The man says, 'Sorry officer I can't do that. I am an
asthmatic. If I do that I'll have a really bad asthma attack.'
'Okay, fine. I need you to come down to the station
to give a blood sample.'
'I can't do that either. I am a haemophiliac.
If I do that, I'll bleed to death.'
'Well, then we need a urine sample.'
'I'm sorry officer I can't do that either. I am also a diabetic.
If I do that I'll get really low blood sugar.'
'Alright then I need you to come out here
and walk this white line.'
'I can't do that, officer.'
'Why not?'
'Because I'm too drunk.'

A policeman pulls a man over for speeding and asks him to get
out of the car. After looking the man over he says,
'Sir, I couldn't help but notice your eyes are bloodshot.
Have you been drinking?'
The man gets really indignant and says,
'Officer, I couldn't help but notice your eyes are glazed.
Have you been eating doughnuts?'

A man who is driving a car is stopped by a police officer.
Officer: 'You were going at least 75 in a 55 zone.'
Man: 'No sir, I was going 60.'
Wife: 'Oh, Harry. You were going 80.'
Officer: 'I'm also going to give you a ticket
for your broken rear light.'
Man: 'Broken rear light? I didn't know about
a broken rear light!'
Wife: 'Oh Harry, you've known
about that rear light for weeks.'

Officer: 'I'm also going to give you a ticket
for not wearing your seat belt.'
Man: 'Oh, I just took it off when you were
walking up to the car.'
Wife: 'Oh, Harry, you never wear your seat belt.'
The man turns to his wife and yells: 'Shut up woman!'
The officer turns to the woman and asks, 'Ma'am, does your
husband talk to you this way all the time?'
Wife: 'No, only when he's drunk.'

A tourist asks a man in uniform, 'Are you a policeman?'
'No, I am an undercover detective.'
'So why are you in uniform?'
'Today is my day off.'

An excited man calls the fire brigade and says,
'Help me, my house is on fire!'
The fireman says, 'Where do you live?'
The man replies, 'I am too excited,
I can't tell you the exact address.'
The fireman asks, 'How do you expect us to get there?'
The man replies, 'What do you mean "how"?
In the big red truck of course!'

A man calls the fire brigade and says, 'Yes, I have just had my
front garden landscaped, I have a nice new flower bed,
a new fish pond with a fountain and a new rose garden.'
'Very nice,' the fireman says, 'but what does that have to do
with the fire service?'
'Well,' the man answers, 'the house next door is on fire and I
don't want you to trample my front garden.'

An agriculture student said to a farmer: 'Your methods are
too old fashioned. I won't be surprised if this tree will give

you less than twenty pounds of apples.'
'I won't be surprised either,' said the farmer.
'This is an orange tree.'

A farmer gets sent to prison, and his wife is trying to keep the
farm together until her husband is released. She's not,
however, very good at farm work, so she writes a letter to him
in jail. 'Dear sweetheart, I want to plant the potatoes.
When is the best time to do it?'
The farmer writes back: 'Honey, don't go near that field.
That's where all my guns are buried.'
Because he is in prison, all the farmer's mail is censored.
So when the prison officers read this, they go to the farm and
dig up the entire potato field looking for guns. After two full
days of digging, they don't find one single weapon.
The farmer then writes to his wife: 'Honey, now is when you
should plant the potatoes.'

**A man was given the job of painting the white lines down
the middle of the road. On his first day he painted six miles;
the next day three miles; the following day less than a mile.
When the foreman asked the man why he kept painting less
each day, he replied, 'I just can't do any better. Each day I
keep getting farther away from the paint can.'**

Three boys are in the school playground, bragging of how
great their fathers are. The first one says, 'Well, my father runs
the fastest. He can fire an arrow, and start to run, I tell you,
and he gets there before the arrow'.
The second one says, 'Ha! You think that's fast! My father is a
hunter. He can shoot his gun and be there before the bullet.'
The third one listens to the other two and shakes his head.
He then says, 'You two know nothing about being fast.
My father is a civil servant. He stops working at 4:30
and he is home by 3:45.'

'I want another room!' said the guest to the hotel owner.
'Why can't you wait until the morning?'
'For one thing, the room is on fire.'

'What would you like me to play?'
said the violin pupil to his teacher.
'Truant.'

'Our teacher talks to herself,' said the boy to his sister.
'So does ours, but she thinks she's talking to us.'

'Jack, what's a fifth of a foot?' asks the teacher.
'A toe?'

'I want to follow my dad's profession when
I leave school,' said the pupil to the careers' teacher.
'What is it exactly you want to become?'
'A detective.'
'So you're dad's a police detective then?'
'No, he's a burglar.'

'Cyril, I'm not happy with your report,' said the teacher.
'I'd take more time over it then.'

'I want you to be quiet. Shakespeare is serious
and not a pantomime!' shouted the drama teacher.
'Oh yes it is!' shouted back the class.

'I want you to be quiet. Shakespeare is serious
and not a pantomime!' shouted the drama teacher.
'And where is my copy of *Macbeth*?'
'It's behind you!'

Why did the history teacher go out every night?
He had plenty of dates.

Why did the PE teacher get sacked from his job?
He wasn't fit for it.

**'Sir, can't you think of anything good to
say about my report?' asked Jack.
'Well I suppose with marks like this
I can't accuse you of cheating.'**

'Jack you've got all the sums wrong in your homework.
I've put a note in your exercise book,' said the maths teacher.
'I wish you hadn't, Dad thought he'd done really well this week.'

**'Did you have a choice of meals at school today?'
asked a mother of her daughter.
'Yes I suppose we did – take it or leave it.'**

'What were your exam results like at school?'
asked the interviewer.
'Underwater.' Replied the job applicant.
'Underwater? What do you mean?'
'Well below C.'

**'I can assure you that we have no problem children
at our school,' said the headmaster to the parents
of a prospective student.
'That's very good, how do you manage that?'
'We exclude them all.'**

'Billy. why are you crying? It's the last day
of school this year,' said the teacher.
'I know, but in five weeks and three days I'll have to come back.'

**'In my day we had corporal punishment at school.
I can only give you detention,' said the teacher.
'Was the corporal very fierce?'**

'Someone threw a stink bomb into the toilets at break,'
moaned the teacher.
'What did it smell like?' asked another teacher.
'A whole lot better.'

**Why did the history teacher go to the supermarket?
He wanted some dates.**

'I made just ten mistakes in my English homework last night,'
said Clare to her mother.
'That's not bad is it?'
'I only wrote one sentence.'

AaBbCc

'I promise you I'll pass
this spelling test, mark
my words,' said the boy
to his teacher.
'If I do you'll fail.'

'My teacher is like tapioca,' said the
boy to his father.
'What, sweet, warm and comforting?'
'No, she makes me feel sick.'

**'You obviously spend too much time
playing computer games at home,' said the
teacher to his short-sighted pupil. 'You should
really get your eyes checked.'
'Checked? I don't think so – I prefer them the
colour they already are.'**

'Do you think your friend can tell me
Napoleon's nationality?' asked the teacher.
'Corsican.'

'Sally can you count to ten?' asked the teacher.
'Yes of course.'
'But can you count any higher?'
'Jack, Queen, King.'

'Every time I turn around you are picking your nose! Why is
that?' said the teacher to the boy.
'Because I'm not allowed to do it at home.'

'We're talking about pets today. Sally do you have a pet?'
asked the teacher.
'Yes, he's called Tiny and he lives in a pond.'
'Why do you call him Tiny?'
'Because he's my newt.'

Is the baker's motto 'Make loaves not war'?

Is a lawyer's motto 'Where there's a will there's a pay'?

Is a motto for judges, 'Try, try and try again'?

**Is a motto for underperforming boxers 'Tis better to have
gloved and lost than never to have gloved at all'?**

'I think I've discovered the hardest piece of
furniture in the world,' said the boy to his teacher.
'What do you mean?'
'The times table.'

Do sports therapists send massages to their friends?

'Excuse me officer, can you tell me the way to Clapham?'
said the American tourist to the policeman.
'Yes, keep your palms straight and slap them together.'

'I have arrested him for dangerous driving. He was doing
55 miles per hour in a 30 mile an hour zone,'
said the policeman to his sergeant.
'What gear was he in?' asked the sergeant.
'A pair of black jeans and a white t-shirt.'

What do you call a crow that joins the police force?
A rookie.

A family have been sitting in a restaurant for a long time,
waiting to be served their Christmas dinner.
Eventually they catch the attention of a waiter.
'Yes sir what can I do for you?' says the waiter.
'Cancel the turkey and bring us all an Easter egg.'

A man is sitting in a fish restaurant, undecided
what to order, when the waiter arrives.
'What are mussels like?' he asks.
'Not bad, I go to the gym every other day.'

A couple have just moved to a new town and ask their next-
door neighbour what a local restaurant is like.
'I wouldn't call it popular,' says the neighbour.
'What's the food like?'
'A bit like a tennis ball.'
'Like a tennis ball, what do you mean?'
'Served but never eaten.'

A man is sitting in a restaurant and he reads on the menu
that the chef will cook anything.
'I'll have a hamster sandwich,' says the customer.
'I bet he can't make me one.'
'Sorry sir, you're absolutely right,
we've just used the last of the bread.'

A man is served the meal of the day in a restaurant
and cannot fathom out what it is.
'What is this?' he asks the waiter.
'It's a bean casserole.'
'I know it's been a casserole, but what is it now?'

A couple have just finished their main course and a waiter
pushes the dessert trolley towards them.
'Genoa cake?' offers the waiter.
'Yes I know what a cake is, but what are those other things?'

Why did the salad go to the psychiatrist?
Because it was mixed up.

Why did the policeman arrest the potato on the motorway?
Because it had broken the spud limit.

Why did the pastry go to the dentist?
To get a filling.

'These mothballs are useless. I want a refund,'
said the customer to the shopkeeper.
'We've never had any complaints before.
What's wrong with them?'
'I've thrown every one at a moth and I haven't hit one all day.'

A farmer runs into a police station and
tells the officer that his pigs have been stolen.
The policeman responded,
'I suspect it is probably a hamburglar.'

'Can you tell me how I get to the Royal Albert Hall?'
asked the American tourist of the policeman.
'I think you'd have to be good
at playing an instrument or something.'

A local baker had an accident.
He fell off his piecycle.

A local dentist has decided to give up dentistry
and grow fruit trees.
He has become an orchardontist.

'My husband died twenty years ago. He was electrocuted
and I can remember his last words,' said the widow.
'What were they?'
'I can fix this.'

A CAT scan technician came into work and said that she was
going out with one of the patients.
Nobody can understand what she saw in him.

Last week an assistant at the local undertakers was sacked.
They had to let him go because he had made
a grave mistake.

What sort of hair do farmers like?
A crop.

Did you hear about the cow farmer that had bandy legs?
He couldn't keep his calves together.

A dancer was giving advice to her children.
Take one step at a time.

'I slipped a disc at the recording studio last week,'
said the singer to the reporter.
'Don't you mean cut a disc?' replied the reporter
'No, I tripped over and hurt my back.'

If a jockey gave up horse racing and took up golf,
could he enter the Ryder Cup?

'What can you tell me about these parrots?'
said the customer to the pet shop owner.
'The parrots speak for themselves.'

A painter was brought in to paint the walls of a church.
He underestimated how many pots of paint he needed and
thinned out the last couple of pots. He met up with the vicar
the following morning and asked whether the job was all right.
The vicar was unhappy with the thinned-down paint and said,
'Repaint and thin no more.'

'Oh NO! There's a man lying in the road in front of us,'
said the driving-school pupil.
'I know, didn't you feel the bump,
you just reversed over him.'

'I'm livid! These tights that you sold me yesterday have got
ladders in them,' complained the customer.
'What do you expect at that price? A marble staircase?'

Why did the footballer shoot himself?
Because there was no one else to pass to.

'I must say you have very small pupils,'
said the optician to his patient.
'I know, I teach in an infants' school.'

'That self-lighting oven that you sold me last week
works beautifully,' said the customer to the shop assistant.
'I'm glad to hear that.'
'Yes, the first time I used it I set fire to myself.'

Does a part-time worker at a funeral director's
only work mournings?

**Librarians are just like betting-shop managers.
They are both bookkeepers.**

'I used to work as a chauffeur but I had to give the job up
when my employer and his wife fell out,'
said the man to his friend.
'That's a shame, but why did you lost your job?'
'Because they fell out of the car.'

Do baggage handlers wear trunks for underwear?

Is a house likely to be draughty
if a builder constructs it with breezeblocks?

**'Did that awful weather damage your greenhouse last night?'
asked the neighbour.
'I'm not sure, I haven't found it yet.'**

Mr Hands was an electrician and all of his four sons
were electricians too. Their motto was,
'Many hands make light work'.

**A woman walked into a butcher's shop
and asked the butcher whether he kept dripping.
'Yes I do behind the counter, but it's not so bad in the freezer.'**

What does a builder use to play computer games?
A joist stick.

**Overnight thieves stole all the slates from a house.
Police warn that the criminals are roofless.**

Gardeners who have not skiied before tend to stay
on the nursery slopes.

**Today a cricketing chef was banned for life
for continually beating the batter.**

After being beaten in the golf tournament by a Spanish player,
Frank Smith shot his opponent.
It was the first time he has made a hole in Juan.

**What's a dietician's favourite song?
'Don't fry for me Argentina'.**

'What do you call trees that lose
their leaves in autumn?'
'Careless?'

**How did the florist die?
She kicked the bouquet.**

What do dentists do when
they go on holiday?
Get someone to fill
in for them.

**A photographer was advising
his son.
'Don't be negative, snap
out of it.'**

A sailor was giving advise
to his son.
'Take it easy, don't take too
much on board.'

**A dairy farmer was asked to give advice to his son.
Trouble is he hadn't herd.**

The funeral service for a local dairy farm was held yesterday.
Following the church service there was a creamation.

**A doctor was giving advice to her son.
'Stay calm and keep your patience.'**

A bus driver was giving advice to his son.
'Life isn't always fare.'

**An actor was giving advice to his son.
'Don't make a scene.'**

A fish was giving advice to its children.
'Cleanliness is next to codliness.'

Do boxers hit the town in their spare time?

Do nurses do needlepoint in their spare time?

Do scientists go fission in their spare time?

Do taxidermists stuff their faces in their spare time?

Do geologists go to rock concerts in their spare time?

How do you take revenge on a travel agent?
Trip him up.

**How do you take revenge on a sewage worker?
Do the dirty on him.**

How do you take revenge on a postman?
Sort him out.

**How do you take revenge on a magician?
Play a trick on him.**

How do you take revenge on a doctor?
Give him a taste of his own medicine.

**How do you take revenge on a burglar?
Get your own back.**

How do you take revenge on a tailor?
Stitch him up.

**How do you take revenge on a gardener?
Turf him out.**

How do you take revenge on a football supporter?
Send him to Coventry.

**How do you take revenge on a sailor?
Deck him.**

How do you take revenge on an underwear salesman?
Sock it to him.

**How do you take revenge on a surgeon?
Cut him out of your will.**

How do you take revenge on a teacher?
Teach him a lesson.

**How do you take revenge on a golfer?
Take a swing at him.**

How do you take revenge on a plumber?
Drop him in hot water.

**How do you take revenge on a carpet fitter?
Floor him.**

How do you take revenge on an electrician?
Shock him.

**How do you take revenge on a mechanic?
Throw a spanner in his works.**

Would you buy a gymnast a tumble drier
for a housewarming present?

**Would you pay for skipping lessons
for a truant for his birthday?**

Would you pay for driving lessons for a
golfer for his birthday?

Do archaeologists drink carbon-dated water?

Last night I went to a party at a soft-drinks manufacturer.
It was a cordial affair.

**Last night I went to a party thrown by an anaesthetist.
It was a gas.**

Last night I went to a party thrown by a mechanic I know.
They played garage all night.

**Last night I went to my bank manager's party.
He insisted on playing musical shares.**

Last night I went to the
fishmonger's party.
He likes to have his friends
around the plaice.

**Last night I went to a
geologist's party.
All there was to drink was
mineral water.**

Last night I had to complain
about the party next door
thrown by a well-
known tennis player.
There was a terrible
racquet all night.

**I wasn't invited to my neighbour's party.
She is a librarian. I suppose it was a hush-hush affair.**

My sister is marrying a fishmonger.
She claims he's quite a catch.

**My sister is marrying a balloon manufacturer.
Last week he popped the question.**

My sister has decided not to marry her mechanic boyfriend.
I think it was quite a wrench.

**My sister is marrying a builder.
She says they needed to cement their relationship.**

My sister is marrying a bus driver.
She reckons he's just the ticket.

Our next-door neighbours are both orthopaedic surgeons
and they're getting married.
Yesterday they opened a joint account.

My sister wanted to marry a waiter, but he had reservations.

**My sister was going to marry a butcher
but she's given him the chop.**

My sister met her boyfriend at the local swimming pool.
I think they're going to take the plunge.

**My sister's in love with a sentry outside Buckingham Palace.
She says he gives her lots of attention.**

My sister wasn't sure about her boyfriend who's a gardener,
but he's grown on her.

**My sister has decided to marry a boxer.
She thinks he's a knockout.**

My sister was going to break up with her boyfriend who's a
rugby player, but he says he'll try harder.

**My sister, the secretary, was going to marry someone from
work, but he decided she wasn't his type.**

My sister has slowly fallen in love with a carpenter.
She says she has learned to love him whittle by whittle.

**My sister is going to marry a perfume salesman.
They've been going out for ages but now
she has the scents to marry him.**

My sister wanted to marry a fireman
but he dumped her and she's quite put out.

**My sister was going to marry an arctic explorer
but he got cold feet.**

My sister actually asked her boyfriend,
who's a toilet attendant, to marry her – but he just flushed.

**My sister is going to marry a telephone engineer.
He's finally given her a ring.**

My sister is going to marry a gymnast.
He had to bend over backwards to persuade her.

**My sister is going to marry a florist.
He has already made all the arrangements.**

My sister is going to marry a judge.
He courted her.

**My sister is going to marry a synchronized swimmer.
She thinks it's a real stroke of luck.**

**My sister is going to marry a butcher.
She's loved him since the day he saved her bacon.**

My sister is going to marry a surveyor.
He reckons no one else measures up to her.

**What kind of car does a wine merchant drive?
A vintage one.**

What kind of car does a lemon grower drive?
A citron.

What kind of car does an electrician drive?
A volts wagon.

What kind of cars do bakers drive?
Rolls.

What kind of cars do shepherds drive?
Lamb drovers.

What kind of car does a barman drive?
A saloon.

What kind of car does a chicken farmer drive?
A hatch back.

What kind of car does a cowboy drive?
Owdi partner.

What kind of car does a railway porter drive?
A station wagon.

What kind of car does a dustman drive?
A pick-up truck.

What kind of car does an inventor drive?
A formula one.

Where do shipbuilders go on holiday?
Hull.

Where do shepherds go on holiday?
Jersey.

Where do fish and chip shop owners go on holiday?
Greece.

Where do drivers go on holiday?
Rhodes.

How do carpenters go on holiday?
In a plane.

How do plumbers go on holiday?
By drain.

What sort of holidays do postmen like?
Package tours.

Where do fishermen go on holiday?
Any plaice will do.

Where do comedians go on holiday?
The Scilly Isles.

'Do you carry sacks of potatoes in this shop?'
'No I get my assistant to carry them.'

'Do you have oxtail?' the customer asked the butcher.
'Of course not, it's only the strings of my apron.'

'Excuse me young man,
do you do anything in small teapots?'
'I haven't done for a very long time madam.'

'Do your eggs all come from a local farmer?'
said the customer to the grocer.
'No they come from hens.'

'Can you throw me that salmon please?'
said the customer in the fishmongers.
'Why do you want me to throw it?'
'So I won't be lying when I tell my wife I caught it.'

'Lay five eggs over there by
the cooker please,'
said the chef to his assistant.
'What do you think I am,
a chicken?'

Yesterday a burglar was arrested
after breaking into a local writer's
home. He faces a long sentence.

Yesterday the local
fishmonger's suffered
a break in.
Police say it was a
smash-and-crab raid.

'I do hope you're not going to wrap my
fish and chips in that newspaper.'
'Why? It won't hurt the food.'
'I've already read that paper.'

'Do you keep stationery?' said the woman in the newsagents.
'I try not to, otherwise my legs get stiff.'

A man dressed in a Batman costume goes into a fishing-
tackle shop and asks for a container of worms.
'What are you going to use these for?' asks the assistant.
'They're not for me, they're for Robin.'

What hand does an ambidextrous chef use to stir the soup?
He doesn't use either, he uses a spoon.

How does an artist relax?
By drawing a bath and painting her nails.

'Can you help me? My dog is like a grandfather clock,'
said the man to the vet.
'Why is that?'
'He's got a round face and ticks.'

'I think you'll find this hotel interesting sir.
It used to be haunted by a ghost. It kept walking up
the stairs during the night.
That's all stopped since we modernized the hotel,'
said the hotel owner to a customer.
'Has the ghost gone?'
'No, it uses the lift.'

'I'm afraid, just as it says on the sign,
I don't give money to people at the door,
even though you're collecting for a charity,' said the old lady.
'Shall I knock on your window then?'

A penniless writer wrote to his friend, telling him that he
couldn't write on an empty stomach. His friend sent back
a pad of notepaper, with a note saying, 'Indeed you cannot
write on an empty stomach, how would you photocopy it?'

Why did the theatre manager give up his job?
Because he wanted a change of scenery.

Why couldn't the architect leave
his children's room at bedtime?
Because they kept asking him for another storey.

A miner decided to give up his job.
It was the pits.

**The casino worker gave up his job
because someone offered him a better deal.**

A novelist decided to give up writing because he'd lost the plot.

**A train driver decided to give up his job,
but he's looking for something else along the same lines.**

A dry cleaner decided to give up his job.
He's already got several pressing appointments.

**A man who worked in a duvet factory decided to give up his
job – it was getting him down.**

A dairy farmer decided to give up his job
but he's looking for an udder one.

**A sword swallower decided to give up his job
because he couldn't see the point anymore.**

A professional swimmer decided to give up his job.
He threw in the towel.

**A farm worker had just finished all the hay baling and
decided to give up his job because this was the last straw.**

A food critic gave up his job
because he had too much on his plate.

**An orchestra conductor gave up his job
because it all went flat.**

A tailor gave up his job because it didn't suit him.

A television DIY presenter gave up his job and didn't know what to do with himshelf anymore.

A man got a new job on a fishing vessel after it was advertised on the Net.

A man gave up making haggis because he didn't have the guts for it anymore.

A man used to work on a chicken farm collecting eggs, but he was laid off.

A rodeo rider was bored with his job and gave it up because he wanted lots of bucks.

A woman gave up her job as an ironer because she was only paid a flat rate.

A man gave up his job as a window cleaner, claiming it was a bit of a pane.

A chicken farmer decided to pack in his job because he only earned a poultry amount.

A telephone engineer decided to give up his job, claiming it was like being an explorer: he went from pole to pole.

Why did the baker stop making donuts?
Because he was tired of the hole business.

**Yesterday our local butcher joined a trade union.
He has become a chop steward.**

A man decided to give up his job as a fishmonger,
claiming it made him shelfish.

A butcher did not give up his job, he was given the chop.

A photographer decided to give up his job because he could
only see the negative side of his work.

**'Excuse me, can I take this train to London?'
asked the man at the railway station.
'Yes I suppose you can, but the driver will be mad
if you go without him.'**

'How long will the next train to London be?'
asks the man at the railway station.
'About the same length as the one that left
about an hour ago.'

**'Can you tell me how far we are from land?'
asked the airline passenger.
'About a mile,' said the air stewardess.**

'What, as the crow flies?'
'No, as the stone falls.'

'Can you tell me where this train is going to?'
said the man at the railway station.
'It's going to London in twenty minutes.'
'That's amazing, the last one I caught took three hours.'

**'We've been in Paris for three days now and I haven't been
to the Louvre yet' said lady to the travel guide.
'You should eat more fruit.'**

Our local electrician rang up
the regional radio station and asked for a plug.

**Our optician has just given up his job because he couldn't
see eye to eye with his customers.**

'What exactly is holding up the train today?' said the
exasperated man at the railway station.
'Wheels and axels as usual sir.'

**'How on earth did you know that I was lying?' said the
burglar as he was arrested.
'That's easy, your lips were moving.'**

'Officer can you tell me whether my indicator lights are
working?' said the driver to the policeman.
'They are, they aren't, they are, they aren't...'

**'Did anybody see who wrote this rude word on the
whiteboard?' said the angry teacher.
'I sincerely hope not, otherwise I'll be in a lot of trouble!'
said Brian.**

'What would you get if you multiplied five by seventeen
and then divided it by three?
Can you answer that Jimmy?' said the teacher.
'No.'

'What time did you wake up
this morning Brian?'
asked the teacher
'About an hour after I got to
school.'

'Do you know if there is
any wildlife
in the arctic Brian?' asked
the teacher
'No I don't think so, it's too
cold for parties.'

'Brian can you tell me what
we do with crude oil?'
sked the teacher.
'Teach it manners?'

'Brian will you stop whistling
while you're working!' said the teacher.
'I'm not working, I'm just whistling.'

'Brian do you know when Rome was built?'
'It was built at night.'
'Strange answer, why?'
'Because I've heard Rome wasn't built in a day.'

'Brian what gives you the idea
that all that Adam and Eve ate was cheese?' asks the teacher.
'I thought they lived in the Garden of Edam.'

**'Brian why are you the only person in class today?'
asked the teacher.
'Because I brought a packed lunch and everyone else ate
school dinners yesterday.'**

'Brian can you tell me the name of the first woman on Earth?'
said the teacher. 'Come on, I'll give you a clue.
Think about an apple.'
'Was it Granny Smith?'

**'Brian can you give me a sentence
that uses the word 'coincide'?' said the teacher.
'If it starts raining and I'm playing in the garden,
my mum tells me to coincide.'**

CROSS-
THE-ROAD
JOKES

Why did the rubber chicken cross the road?
She wanted to stretch her legs.

**Why did the Roman chicken cross the road?
She was afraid someone would Caesar.**

Why did the chicken cross the road?
To prove to the hedgehog that it could be done.

**Why did Douglas Adams' chicken cross the road?
42.**

Why did Salvador Dali's chicken cross the road?
A fish.

**Why did Homer Simpson's chicken cross the road?
Because there was free beer on the other side.**

Why did William Shakespeare's chicken cross the road?
To cross or not to cross – that is the question.

**Why did Captain Kirk's chicken cross the road?
To boldly go where no chicken has gone before.**

Why did the chicken cross the road?
It had a death wish.

**Why didn't the chicken cross the road?
It was having a day off.**

Why did the turtle cross the road?
Because the chicken was on holiday.

**Why did the chicken cross the football pitch?
He heard the referee calling fowl.**

Why did the chicken cross the road?
To spread a global pandemic.

**Why did the chicken cross the road?
Because the underpass hadn't been built yet.**

Why did the chicken cross the road,
roll in the mud and then cross the road again?
Because he was a dirty double-crosser.

**Why did the psychic chicken cross the road?
To get in touch with the other side.**

Why did the chicken cross the road?
It wanted to see a man lay a brick.

Why did the chicken cross the playground?
To get to the other slide.

**Why did the dinosaur
cross the road?
Chickens hadn't evolved yet.**

Why did the cow cross the
road?
To get to the udder side.

Why did the sheep
cross the road?
To get to the baa baa shop to have a haircut.

Why did the dog cross the road?
To find a barking space.
Why did the turtle cross the road?
To get to the shell petrol station.

Why did the horse cross the road?
To get to his naybourhood.

Why did the skeleton cross the road alone?
Because he had no body to cross with him.

Why did the one-handed skeleton
cross the road?
To get the second-hand shop.

Why did the orange stop
in the middle of the road?
Because he ran out of juice.

Why did the leech cross the road?
He was stuck to the chicken.

Why did the chicken cross the road?
Because the rooster egged her on.

Why did the hedgehog cross the road?
To see his flatmate.

Why did the alligator cross the road?
Because he was following the chicken.

Why did the old man cross the road?
To look at his life from the other side.

Why was the cat afraid to cross the road?
Because he was a scaredy cat.

Why did the rabbit cross the road?
To get to the hare salon.

Why did the snail cross the road?
Don't know – he hasn't got there yet.

Why did the bubble gum cross the road?
Because it was stuck to the chicken's foot.

Why did the spider cross the road?
To get to her website.

How did the wealthy chicken cross the road?
In her stretch limousine.

Why did the Baldrick's chicken cross the road?
Because it had a cunning plan.

Why did Darth Vader's chicken cross the road?
Because it couldn't resist the power of the dark side.

Why did the nun's chicken cross the road?
It did it out of habit.

Why did Neil Armstrong's chicken cross the road?
Because it was one small step for chicken kind and one
giant leap for poultry.

Why did Bob Dylan's chicken cross the road?
How many roads must a wise chicken walk down?

Why did Einstein's chicken cross the road?
Did the chicken really cross the road
or did the road move beneath the chicken?
Why did the cow cross the road?
To go to the moooovies

Why did the little boy cross the road?
To get to the other slide.

Why did the banana cross the road?
It was a slip road.

Why did the pig cross the road?
Because it was a road hog.

Why did the lion cross the road?
Because it wasn't a mane road.

Why did the penguin cross the road?
Because it was an ice day.

Why did the chicken cross the road?
Because of the fowl weather.

Why did the dog cross the road?
That is a bone of contention.

Why didn't the needle-less hedgehog cross the road?
Because he was spineless.

Why did the monkey cross the road?
He always would, gibbon the chance.

Why did the snake cross the road?
Because it was hissing with rain.

Why did the squirrel cross the road?
Because it was nuts.
Why did the chicken cross the road?
To get away from the bagpipe recital.

Why did the crocodile cross the road?
Because it was chasing the chicken.

Why did the computer cross the road?
Because the chicken programmed it to do so.

Why did the shepherd cross the road?
To prove he wasn't sheepish.

Why did the A cross the road?
Because there was a B behind her.

**Why did the punk cross the road?
Because he had stapled himself to the chicken.**

Why did the clown cross the road?
To find his rubber chicken.

**Why did the chicken cross the road
and head for Switzerland?
It wanted to go yokelling.**

Why did the chicken pretend to cross the road?
Because it was a practical yoker.

Why did the pirate's phone go beep, beep, beep, beep
as he crossed the road?
Because he had left it off the hook.

Why didn't the skeleton cross the road?
He didn't have the guts.

Why did the hamburger cross the road?
To ketchup with the French fries.

What time did the chicken cross the road?
5 o'cluck.

Why did the crocodile cross the road?
It wanted to play snap with the chicken.

Why didn't the car cross the road?
Because it had turned into a driveway.

Why couldn't the oak tree cross the road?
Because it had acorn.

What happened to the magic tractor
when it crossed the road?
It turned into a field.

Why didn't the flower cross the road?
Because it was in bed.

Why did the cow cross the road?
To get to the Milky Way.

Why did the hairdresser cross the road?
Because he wanted to take a short cut.

Why did the duck cross the road?
It needed to pay a bill.

Why did the chicken from Prague cross the road?
It wanted to cash a Czech.

Why did the Italian chicken cross the road?
It was just Roming around.

Why did the wizard cross the road?
He wanted to learn to spell.

Why did the bee cross the road?
To get to the buzz stop.

Why did the calendar cross the road?
Because his days were numbered.

Why did the laughing flamingo cross the road?
Because somebody had tickled it pink.

Why did the elephant cross the road?
Because he wanted to make a trunk call.

Why did the cigar cross the road?
It wanted to see the match.

Why didn't the needle cross the road?
It couldn't see the point.

Why did the chicken cross the road?
Because it was poultry in motion.

Why did the comedian cross the road?
He just did it for a laugh.

**Why did the fish cross the road?
To get across to the other tide.**

Why did the fish cross the road?
It didn't want to be late for shoal.

**Why did the poet cross the road backwards?
Because he wanted to write in reverse.**

What happened when the cricketer crossed the road?
He was bowled over.

Why did the mathematician cross the road?
Because he had a lot of problems to solve.

What did the beaver say when he couldn't cross the road?
Dam.

Why did the duck cross the road upside down?
He didn't want to quack up.

Why didn't the mask cross the road?
He couldn't face it.

Why did the biscuit cross the road?
Because he felt crummy.

Why did the 0 cross the road?
To tell the 8 he liked his belt.

FAMILY AND RELATIONSHIP JOKES

Three men were talking in a pub. Two of them were talking
about the amount of control they had over their wives, while
the third remained strangely quiet. After a while one of the
first two turned to the third and said, 'Well, what about you,
what sort of control do you have over your wife?'
The third fellow said, 'I'll tell you. Just the other night my wife
came to me on her hands and knees.'
'Wow! What happened then?' The third man took a healthy
swallow of his beer, sighed and uttered, 'She said, "Get out
from under the bed and fight like a man".'

**Bill: I was sorry to hear that your mother-in-law died.
What was the complaint?
George: We haven't had any yet.**

Once upon a time, two women were talking and the one asked
the other how many times she's been married.
The answer was four.
'Four times!' exclaimed the first woman.
'Why so many?'
So the other woman said, 'Well, I
first got married when I was very
young, and I married this
wonderful man who was a
banker. However, one day just
a few weeks after we were
married, his bank was robbed and
he was shot and killed.'
'Oh my, that's terrible,' the first
woman said.
'Well, it wasn't so tragic.
Soon after that, I started
seeing another man who
performed in the circus. He
was really a great guy, but

he lived pretty dangerously because he performed his high-wire act without a net. Well, a few weeks after we got married, he was performing a show and suddenly a gust of wind came by and knocked him off his wire and he was killed.'
'Your second husband was killed too? That's horrible!'
'Yes, it was terrible, but at the funeral I fell in love with the minister and we got married soon after that. Unfortunately, one Sunday while he was walking to church, he was hit by a car and killed.'
'Three? Three husbands of yours were killed? How could you live through all that?'
'It was pretty tough, but then I met my present husband. And he's a wonderful man. I think we'll live a long, happy life together.'
'And what does your present husband do for a living?'
'He's a funeral director.'
'A funeral director? I don't understand something here. First you marry a banker, then a circus performer, then a minister, and now a mortician? Why such a weird group of husbands?'
'Well, if you think about it it's not too hard to understand:
One for the money...
Two for the show...
Three to get ready...
And four to go!'

What's the difference between a girlfriend and wife?
45 lbs.

What's the difference between a boyfriend and husband?
45 minutes.

My wife had a go at me last night. She said 'You'll drive me to my grave'. I had the car out in 30 seconds.

I got home from work and my wife said, 'I'm very sorry dear,
but the cat's eaten your dinner'.
I said, 'Don't worry – I'll get you a new cat'.

**I was cleaning out the attic the other day with my wife.
Filthy, dirty and covered with cobwebs –
but she's good with the kids.**

A man gets home from work one evening to find his blonde
wife sitting at the kitchen table still in her dressing gown.
She has emptied a box of cornflakes all over the table
and is staring at them intently.
Worried the man asks her what's wrong.
'It's awful.' she replies 'I've been trying to do this
jigsaw all day and I still can't get it to look
like the picture on the box!'

Men are like weather – nothing can be done to change them.

Men are like blenders – you need one,
but you're not quite sure why.

**Men are like chocolate bars – sweet, smooth, and they
usually head right for your hips.**

Men are like commercials – you can't believe a word they say.

**Men are like mascara – they usually run at the
first sign of emotion.**

Men are like lava lamps – fun to look at, but not very bright.

**Men are like parking places – all the good ones are taken,
and the rest are handicapped.**

If it's true that girls are inclined to marry men like their
fathers, it is understandable why so many mothers
cry so much at weddings.

Once there was a millionaire, who collected live alligators.
He kept them in the pool in back of his mansion.
The millionaire also had a beautiful daughter
who was single. One day he decided to throw a huge party,
and during the party he announced, 'My dear guests ...
I have a proposition to every man here. I will give one
million dollars or my daughter to the man who can swim
across this pool full of alligators and emerge alive!'
As soon as he finished his last word, there was the sound of
a large splash! There was one guy in the pool swimming
with all his might and screaming with fear. The crowd
cheered him on as he kept stroking as though he was
running for his life. Finally, he made it to the other side
with only a torn shirt and some minor injuries.
The millionaire was impressed.
He said, 'My boy that was incredible! Fantastic! I didn't
think it could be done! Well I must keep my end of the
bargain. Do you want my daughter or the one million dollars?'
The guy says, 'Listen, I don't want your money, nor do I
want your daughter! I want the person who pushed me in
that water!'

A newlywed wife said to her husband when he returned from
work, 'I have great news for you. Pretty soon, we're going to be
three in this house instead of two.'
Her husband ran to her with a smile on his face and delight in
his eyes. He was glowing with happiness and kissing his wife
when she said, 'I'm glad that you feel this way.
Mother moves in tomorrow.'

Laura tells her husband, 'Stuart, that young couple that just moved in next door seem such a loving twosome. Every morning, when he leaves the house, he kisses her goodbye, and every evening when he comes homes, he brings her a dozen roses. Now, why can't you do that?'
'I don't think so,' Stuart replies. 'I hardly know the girl.'

Mary and Jane are old friends. They have both been married to their husbands for a long time. Mary is upset because she thinks her husband doesn't find her attractive anymore.
'As I get older he doesn't bother to look at me!' Mary cries.
'I'm so sorry for you. As I get older my husband says I get more beautiful every day,' replied Jane.
To which Mary responded, 'Yes, but your husband's an antique dealer!'

A man asked his friend why he had never been married.
Replied the friend, 'Well, I suppose I just never met the right woman. I have been looking for the perfect girl.'
'Oh, come on now,' said his friend. 'Surely you've met at least one girl that you wanted to marry.'
'Yes, there was a girl, once. I guess she was the one perfect girl – the only perfect girl I really ever met. She was just the right everything. I really mean that she was the perfect girl for me,' replied the friend.
'Well, why didn't you marry her?' asked the man.
'She was looking for the perfect man.'

What is the difference between a man and a chimpanzee?
One is hairy, smelly, and is always scratching his bum.
And, the other is a chimpanzee.

Wanting to lose weight, a woman placed a picture of a shapely, pinup model in her refrigerator to remind her of her goal. The reminder worked like a charm as the woman discovered that she had lost 10 pounds in the first month of using this method. The downside to this was that her husband spent so much time going into the fridge to look at the picture that he ended up gaining 15 pounds.

A wife noticed her husband standing on the bathroom scales, sucking in his stomach. Thinking that he was trying to weigh less with this manoeuvre, she commented,
'I don't think that is going to help.'
'Of course it does,' he said. 'It's the only way that I can see the numbers.'

One Tuesday evening, two confirmed bachelors were talking when the conversation eventually drifted from sports to politics, and then on to cooking.
The first guy said, 'I got a cookbook once, but I could never do anything with it.'
'Too much fancy stuff in it, eh?' asked the other bachelor.
'You said it,' the first guy replied. 'Every one of those recipes began the same way, 'Take a clean dish...'

What is the difference between a new husband and a new dog?
After a year, the dog is still excited to see you.

Why do bachelors like smart women?
Opposites attract.

What is the difference between a man and E.T.?
E.T. phoned home.

How many men does it take to put the toilet seat down?
Nobody knows, it hasn't happened yet.

Why is it hard for women to find men who are sensitive,
caring and good looking?
Because those men already have boyfriends.

**Why does it take longer
to build a snowman than
a snow woman?
Because it takes so long to
hollow out the man's head.**

Two mothers were talking about
their sons. The first said, 'My son is
such a saint. He works hard,
doesn't smoke, and he hasn't
so much as looked at a woman
in over two years.'
The other woman said, 'Well, my
son is a saint himself. Not only
has he not looked at a woman
in over three years, but he
hasn't touched a drop of liquor
in all that time.'
'My word,' the first mother
said. 'You must be so proud.'
I am,' the second mother replied.
'And when he's paroled next month,
I'm going to throw him a big party.'

**A childless couple decide to adopt a Spanish baby. After the
adoption they enrol on a Spanish language course. The tutor
asks them why they had enrolled and the man replies,
'When the baby begins to talk we'll understand him.'**

A man who lived in an apartment block put his head out of
the window to see if it was raining. As he did so, a glass eye fell

into his hand. He looked up and saw a young woman leaning
over the balcony above him. 'Is this yours?' he asked.
'Yes,' she replied, 'could you bring it up for me?'
The man took the eye to her apartment and she was very
grateful and offered him a drink. They chatted away and she
asked him to join her for dinner, which he agreed to do.
Later, she said, 'I've had a marvellous evening,
would you like to stay the night?'
'Do you behave like this with every man you meet?'
the man asked.
'No,' replied the woman. 'Only those who catch my eye.'

A young boy and his father from the countryside were
visiting a city for the first time. They were amazed by almost
everything they saw, but especially by two shiny silver walls
that moved apart and back together again by themselves.
The boy asked, 'What is this, Father?'
The father, who had never seen a lift before, responded,
'I have no idea what it is'.
While the boy and his father were watching wide-eyed,
an old lady in a wheelchair rolled up to the moving walls
and pressed a button. The walls opened and the lady rolled
between them into a small room. The walls closed and the
boy and his father watched as small circles lit up above the
walls. The walls opened up again and a beautiful woman
stepped out. The father looked at his son and said,
'Go get your mother'.

A husband was sitting at his dying wife's side.
'Sleep now, it's all right,' he told her.
But she kept trying to sit up and said, 'Honey, I really need to
tell you something.' Finally the husband let her get it off her
chest. 'I need to tell you something before I die.
During the last two months, I slept with your brother,
your best friend and your father.'

'Don't worry about it,' the husband said,
'I already know. Why do you think I poisoned you?'

A woman announces to her friend that she is getting married
for the fourth time. 'How wonderful! But I hope you don't
mind me asking what happened to your first husband?'
'He ate poisonous mushrooms and died.'
'Oh, how tragic! What about your second husband?'
'He ate poisonous mushrooms too and died.'
'Oh, how terrible! I'm almost afraid to ask you about your
third husband.'
'He died of a broken neck.'
'A broken neck?'
'Yes. He wouldn't eat the mushrooms.'

Why do most women pay more attention
to their appearance than improving their minds?
Because most men are stupid but few are blind.

A husband and wife had four boys. The older three had red
hair, light skin, and were tall, while the youngest son had
black hair, dark eyes, and was short. The father eventually
took ill and was lying on his deathbed when he turned to his
wife and said, 'Before I die, be totally honest with me –
is our youngest son my child?'
The wife replied, 'I swear on everything
that's holy that he is your son.'
With that the husband passed away. The wife muttered,
'Thank God he didn't ask about the other three'.

If you love something, set it free. If it comes back, it will always
be yours. If it never returns, it was never yours to begin with.
If it just sits in your living room, eats your food, messes up your
stuff, takes your money, and behaves as if you never set it free
in the first place, then you either married or gave birth to it.

A man walks into a bar one night, goes up to the barman,
and asks for a beer. 'Certainly, sir, that'll be one penny.'
'One penny!' exclaimed the customer.
'That's right.' The barman replied.
So the customer glanced over at the menu, and asked,
'Could I have a nice juicy T-bone steak, with fries,
peas and a salad?'
'Certainly sir,' replied the bartender. 'That'll be four pence.'
'Four pence! Where's the owner?'
The barman replied, 'Upstairs with my wife.'
'What's he doing with your wife?'
The bartender smiled.
'Same as what I'm doing to his business.'

What did Christopher Columbus's mother say?
'I don't care what you've discovered Christopher,
you still could have written.'

What did Michelangelo's mother say?
'Mike, can't you paint the walls like other children? Do you
have any idea how hard it is to get that stuff off the ceiling?'

A husband and wife were at a party chatting with some friends
when the subject of marriage counselling came up.
'Oh, we'll never need that. My husband and I have a great
relationship,' the wife explained. 'He studied communications
at university and I specialized in theatre arts.
He communicates well and I just act like I'm listening.'

Man: 'Your place or mine?'
Woman: 'Both. You go to yours, and I'll go to mine.'

A man comes home from work and finds his wife admiring her
breasts in the mirror. The husband asks, 'What are you doing?'

She replies, 'I went to the doctor today, and he told me I have the breasts of a twenty-five-year-old.'
The husband retorts, 'Well, what did he say about your fifty-year-old bum?'
'I'm sorry dear, your name never came up.'

First man (proudly): 'My wife is an angel!'
Second man: 'You're lucky – mine's still alive.'

A married couple had a terrible accident. The woman's face was burned severely. The doctor told the husband they couldn't graft any skin from her body because she was so thin. The husband donated some of his skin. However, the only place suitable was from his buttocks.
The husband requested that no one be told of this, because, after all, it was a very delicate matter.
After the surgery was completed, everyone was astounded at the woman's new beauty. She looked more radiant than she ever did before. All her friends and relatives just ranted and raved at her youthful beauty.
She was alone with her husband one day, and she wanted to thank him for what he did. She said, 'Dear, I just want to thank you for everything you did for me.
There is no way I could ever repay you.'
The husband replied, 'Oh don't worry, I get thanks enough every time your mother comes over and kisses your cheek!'

There was an expectant father who had spent quite some time waiting for the offspring to arrive at his in-laws' house. He tells his father-in-law, 'When my son comes, do not call up my office and say that I have become a father of a boy because I'll have to shell out a lot for parties. Just leave me a message that the clock has arrived.
This will be our code for the arrival of the baby.'
The offspring does finally arrive one day, but it's a daughter.

The father-in-law now thinks to himself, 'If I tell him that the clock has not arrived, he'll misunderstand and think that something has happened to the baby and come rushing over.'
So the father-in-law left the following message:
'The clock has arrived, but the pendulum is missing.'

What is the definition of mixed emotions?
Watching your mother-in-law go off
a cliff in your new Mercedes.

A man walks into a shoe shop and asks for a pair of size 8 lace-up shoes. The salesman says, 'But, sir, I can see from here you're at least a size 11.'
The man says, 'Just bring me a size 8 tie shoe.'
The salesman brings them, the man stuffs his feet into them, ties them tight, and then he stands up, obviously in pain.
The salesman just has to ask, 'Sir, why must you have these undersized shoes?'
The man replies, 'I lost my business and my house, I live with my mother-in-law, my wife is having an affair with my best friend, my daughter is pregnant, and my son is gay. The only pleasure I have in life is taking off these damn shoes.

In her own eyes, Julia was the most popular girl around.
'A lot of men are going to be totally miserable when I marry.'
'Really?' said her date, 'And just how many men are you intending to marry?'

Why do women have smaller feet than men?
It's one of those 'evolutionary' things that allows them to stand closer to the kitchen sink.

How do you repair a woman's watch?
You don't need to. There is a clock on the oven.

Why are well-dressed men always married?
Because their wife chooses their clothes for them.

What do you call a man with only half a brain?
Gifted.

How many honest, intelligent, caring men in the world
does it take to do the dishes?
Both of them.

Why are most jokes so short?
So men can remember them.

What do they call a woman who works as hard as a man?
Lazy.

'How would you like to pay?' asked the cashier, after bagging items the woman wished to purchase. As she fumbled for her wallet the cashier noticed a TV remote in her purse. 'So, do you always carry your TV remote?' the cashier asked.
'No,' she replied, 'but my husband refused to come shopping with me, so I figured this was the most legal evil thing I could do to him.'

Men spend thousands of pounds on tools because they have learned that, unlike a woman's love and devotion, tools have a lifetime guarantee.

When you hear a man boast that he is the boss
in his own house, you can be sure that
he might also lie about other things.

**I know I'm not going to understand women.
I'll never understand how you can take boiling hot wax,
pour it on to your upper thigh, rip the hair out by the roots,
and still be afraid of a spider.**

A man had six children and was very proud of his
achievement. He was so proud of himself that he started
calling his wife, 'Mother of Six,' in spite of her objections.
One night they went to a party. The man decided that it was
time to go home, and wanted to find out if his wife is ready to
leave as well. He shouted at the top of his voice,
'Shall we go home, Mother of Six?'
His wife, irritated by her husband's lack of discretion shouted
back, 'Anytime you're ready, Father of Four!'

TEN POLITICALLY CORRECT TERMS FOR MALES
**He does not have a beer gut.
He develops a 'Liquid Grain Storage Facility'.**
He is not quiet.
He is a 'Conversational Minimalist'.
**He is not stupid.
He suffers from 'Minimal Cranial Development'.**
He does not get lost all the time.
He 'Discovers Alternative Destinations'.
**He is not balding.
He is in 'Follicle Regression'.**
You do not buy him a drink.
You initiate an 'Alcohol-for-Conversation Exchange'.
**You do not kiss him.
You become 'Facially Conjoined'.**

He does not get falling-down drunk.
He becomes 'Accidentally Horizontal'.
He does not constantly talk about cars.
He has a 'Vehicular Addiction'.
He is not unsophisticated.
He is 'Socially Malformed'.

Why is it dangerous to let your man's mind wander?
It's too small to be out alone.

I asked my wife the other day what she liked best about my
firm, trim body, my intellect or me.
She said, 'Your sense of humour'.

On their 40th wedding anniversary and during the banquet
celebrating it, Tom was asked to give his friends a brief
account of the benefits of a marriage of such long duration.
'Tell us Tom, just what is it you have learned from all those
wonderful years with your wife?'
Tom responds, 'Well, I've learned that marriage is the best
teacher of all. It teaches you loyalty, forbearance, meekness,
self-restraint, forgiveness and a great many other qualities
you wouldn't have needed if you'd stayed single.'

A man was invited for dinner at a friend's house. Every time the
host needed something, he preceded his request to his wife by
calling her 'My Love', 'Darling', 'Sweetheart', etc. His friend
looked at him and said, 'That's really nice after all of these
years you've been married to keep saying those little pet names.'
The host said, 'Well, honestly, I've forgotten her name.'

Why do men chase women
they have no intention of marrying?
For the same reason dogs chase cars
they have no intention of driving.

What is gross stupidity?
144 men in one room.

How do men sort their washing?
'Filthy' and 'Filthy but Wearable'.

What do men and beer have in common?
They're both empty from the neck up.

What's the difference between a man and Bigfoot?
One is covered with matted hair and smells awful.
The other has big feet.

Jill and John got married. John was determined it would be a
marriage of equals. So, the first morning back from their
honeymoon, he brought Jill breakfast in bed.
Jill wasn't impressed with his culinary skills, however.
She looked disdainfully at the tray, and snorted, 'Poached?
I wanted scrambled!' Undaunted, the next morning John
brought his true love a scrambled egg.
Jill wasn't having any of it. 'Do you think I don't like variety?
I wanted poached this morning!'
Determined to please Jill, the next morning he thought,
'Third time lucky' and brought her two eggs, one scrambled
and one poached.
'Here, my love, enjoy!' Jill looked at the plate and said,
'You scrambled the wrong egg.'

'Ever since we got married, my wife has tried to change me.
She got me to stop drinking, smoking and running around
until all hours of the night. She taught me how to dress
well, enjoy the fine arts, gourmet cooking, classical music,
even how to invest,' said the man.

'Sounds like you may be bitter because she changed you so drastically,' remarked his friend.
'I'm not bitter. Now that I'm so improved, she just isn't good enough for me.'

The doorbell rang this morning. When I opened the door, there was my mother-in-law on the front step.
She said, 'Can I stay here for a few days?'
I said, 'Sure you can.' And shut the door in her face.

A husband was in big trouble when he forgot his wedding anniversary. His wife told him 'Tomorrow there better be something in the driveway for me that goes zero to 200 in two seconds flat. The next morning the wife found a small package in the driveway. She opened it and found a brand new bathroom scales.

There is a new Barbie that's just been released.
It is called, 'Divorcé Barbie'.
It comes complete with all Ken's accessories!

FIVE DIFFERENCES BETWEEN MEN AND WOMEN
A man will pay £2 for a £1 item he wants.
A woman will pay £1 for a £2 item that she doesn't want.
A woman worries about the future until she gets a husband.
A man never worries about the future until he gets a wife.
A successful man is one who makes more money than his wife can spend. A successful woman is one who can find such a man.
To be happy with a man you must understand him a lot and love him a little. To be happy with a woman you must love her a lot and not try to understand her at all.
Married men live longer than single men – but married men are a lot more willing to die.

FIVE MORE DIFFERENCES BETWEEN
MEN AND WOMEN

Any married man should forget his mistakes –
there's no use in two people remembering the same thing.

**Men wake up as good-looking as they went to bed.
Women somehow deteriorate during the night.**

A woman marries a man expecting he will change,
but he doesn't.
A man marries a woman expecting
that she won't change and she does.

**A woman has the last word in any argument. Anything a
man says after that is the beginning of a new argument.**

There are only two times when a man doesn't understand a
woman – before marriage and after marriage.

A woman accompanied her husband to see his doctor. After
his check-up, the doctor called the wife into his office alone.
'Your husband is suffering from a very severe stress disorder.
If you don't do the following, your husband will surely die.
Each morning, make him a healthy breakfast. Be pleasant at
all times. For lunch make him a nutritious meal.
For dinner prepare an especially nice meal for him. Don't
burden him with chores. Don't discuss your problems with
him; it will only make his stress worse. No nagging. If you
can do this for the next ten months to a year,
I think your husband will regain his health completely.'
On the way home, the husband asked his wife.
'What did the doctor say?'
'He said you're going to die,' she replied.

A man walked into the ladies clothes section of a department
store, walked up to the woman behind the counter and said,
'I'd like to buy a bra for my wife'
What type of bra?' asked the clerk.

'Type?' inquires the man. 'There is more than one type?'
'Look around,' said the saleslady, as she showed a sea of bras
in every shape, size, colour and material. 'Actually, even with
all of this variety, there are really only three types of bras,'
replied the salesclerk.
Confused, the man asked what the types were.
The saleslady replied 'The Catholic type, the, Salvation Army
type, and the Baptist type. Which one do you need?'
Still confused the man asked,
'What is the difference between them?'
The lady responded, 'It is all really quite simple. The Catholic
type supports the masses, the Salvation Army type lifts up the
fallen, and the Baptist type makes mountains out of mole hills.'

FIVE PUT DOWNS
Man: Is this seat empty?
Woman: Yes, and this one will be if you sit down.
Man: How do you like your eggs in the morning?
Woman: Unfertilised.
Man: I would go to the end of the world for you.
Woman: But would you stay there?
Man: If I could see you naked, I'd die happy.
Woman: If I saw you naked, I'd probably die laughing.
Man: So, what do you do for a living?
Woman: I'm a female impersonator.

Betty's mother was visiting her daughter and son-in-law Bill.
Bill came home from work and found six vacuum-cleaner
salesmen outside his house.
He dashed in and said, 'Mum, there are six men outside who
all claim they have an appointment for
a vacuum cleaner demonstration!'
'That's right,' the mother-in-law replied. 'Now you just show
them all to different rooms and let them start demonstrating.'

Two men were in a pub. One man said, 'Did you know that
beer contains female hormones?'
The other man said, 'No! Is it true?'
'Yes,' said the first man. 'If you drink too much, you start
talking rubbish and you drive terribly.'

Yesterday I bought a coconut for my 16-year-old daughter.
I then realized we have been living too long, too far away from
nature. She said: 'This white stuff inside smells like shampoo.'

What is the difference between out-laws, and in-laws?
Out-laws are wanted.

Losing a husband can be hard.
In my case, it was almost impossible.

There is a man who goes out drinking all the time and
comes home very later every night. One night his wife
decides to teach him a lesson, so she dresses up like
Satan and decides to hide in the dark and scare him when
he gets home. So the man comes home and his wife jumps
out and screams in his face. He just looks at her and says,
'You don't scare me – I'm married to your sister!'

Some mornings I wake up grouchy
and on others I just let her sleep!

TRANSLATING MALE SAYINGS
'I'm going fishing' really means: 'I'm going to drink myself
dangerously stupid and stand by a stream with a stick in my
hand, while the fish swim by in complete safety.'
'It's a guy thing' really means: 'There is no rational thought
pattern connected with it, and you have no chance at all of
making it logical.'

'Can I help with dinner?' really means: 'Why isn't it already on the table?'
'Uh huh' or 'Yes, dear' really means: Absolutely nothing. It's a conditioned response.
'It would take too long to explain' really means: 'I have no idea how it works.'

MORE MALE TRANSLATIONS
'I'm getting more exercise lately' really means: 'The batteries in the remote are dead.'
'We're going to be late' really means: 'Now I have a legitimate excuse to drive like a maniac.'
'Take a break, honey, you're working too hard' really means: 'I can't hear the game over the vacuum cleaner.'
'That's interesting, dear' really means: 'Are you still talking?'
'We don't need material things to prove our love' really means: 'I forgot our anniversary again.'

EVEN MORE MALE TRANSLATIONS
'I can't find it' really means: 'It didn't fall into my outstretched hands, so I'm completely clueless.'
'Oh, don't fuss. I just cut myself, it's no big deal.' really means: 'I have severed a limb, but will bleed to death before I admit I'm hurt.'
'I do help around the house' really means: 'I once put a dirty towel in the washing basket.'
'I've got my reasons for what I'm doing' really means: 'I sure hope I think of some reasons pretty soon.'
'What did I do this time?' really means: 'What did you catch me doing?'

FINAL MALE TRANSLATIONS
'I heard you' really means: 'I haven't the foggiest clue what you just said, and I'm hoping desperately that I can fake it.'
'You look terrific' really means: 'Oh, God, please don't try on one more outfit. I'm starving.'
'I missed you' really means: 'I can't find my sock drawer, the kids are hungry and we are out of toilet paper.'
'I'm not lost. I know exactly where we are.' really means: 'I'm lost. I have no idea where we are, and no one will ever see us alive again.'
'I don't need to read the instructions' really means: 'I am perfectly capable of mucking it up without printed help.'

**Why do women wear white on their wedding day?
All major kitchen appliances come in white.**

Why do wives live longer than their husbands?
Because they aren't married to women!

**Why did the woman cross the road?
Never mind that – what's she doing out of the kitchen.**

TRANSLATIONS OF WOMEN'S LANGUAGE
'Yes' = 'No'
'No' = 'Yes'
'Maybe' = 'No'
'I'm sorry' = 'You'll be sorry'
'We need' = 'I want'

**MORE TRANSLATIONS OF WOMEN'S LANGUAGE
'It's your decision' = 'The correct decision should be obvious by now'**
'Do what you want' = 'You'll pay for this later'
'We need to talk' = 'I need to complain'

'Go ahead' = 'I don't want you to'
'I'm not upset' = 'Of course I'm upset, you insensitive idiot!'

EVEN MORE FEMALE TRANSLATIONS
'You're so manly' = 'You need a shave and you sweat a lot'
'This kitchen is so inconvenient' = 'I want a new house'
'I want new curtains' = 'And carpeting, and furniture,
and wallpaper'
'I heard a noise' = 'I noticed you were almost asleep'
'Do you love me?' = 'I'm going to ask for something expensive'
**'How much do you love me?' = 'I did something today
you're really not going to like'**

**Marriage is very much like a violin; after the sweet music is
over, the strings are attached.**

Marriage is not a word – it's a sentence. A life sentence.

**Marriage is not just a having a wife,
but also worries inherited forever.**

Marriage is love. Love is blind.
Therefore, marriage is an institution for the blind.

**Marriage is a thing that puts a ring on a woman's finger
and two under the man's eyes.**

Marriage certificate is just another word for a work permit.

**Marriage requires a man to prepare four types of 'rings':
The Engagement Ring
The Wedding Ring
The Suffe-Ring
The Endu-Ring**

Getting married is very much like going to the restaurant with friends. You order what you want, and when you see what the other fellow has, you wish you had ordered that.

There was a man who muttered a few words in the church and found himself married. A year later he muttered something in his sleep and found himself divorced.

Son: 'How much does it cost to get married, Dad?'
Father: 'I don't know son, I'm still paying for it.'

**Son: 'Is it true that in ancient China, a man didn't know his wife until he married.'
Father: 'That happens everywhere, son, everywhere.'**

A gentleman is one who never swears at his wife while ladies are present.

A husband is living proof that a wife can take a joke.

When a newly married man looks happy, we know why. But when a ten-year married man looks happy, we wonder why.

Don't marry for money; you can borrow it cheaper elsewhere.

Feminists are okay, I just wouldn't want my sister to marry one.

If all men were brothers, would you let one marry your sister?

If your wife wants to learn how to drive, don't stand in her way.

In marriage, as in war, it is permitted to take every advantage of the enemy.

In marriage, the bride gets a shower.
But for the groom, it's curtains!

One night a wife found her husband standing over their baby's crib. Silently she watched him. As he stood looking down at the sleeping infant, she saw on his face a mixture of emotions: disbelief, doubt, delight, amazement, enchantment, scepticism.
Touched by this unusual display and the deep emotions it aroused, with eyes glistening she slipped her arm around her husband. 'A penny for your thoughts,' she said.
'It's amazing!' he replied. 'I just can't see how anybody can make a crib like that for thirty quid.'

Love thy neighbour, but make sure her husband is away first.

Love: an obsessive delusion that is cured by marriage.

Many a wife thinks her husband is the world's greatest lover.
But she can never catch him at it.

Marriage is a mutual relationship if both parties know when to be mute.

Marriage is a rest period between romances.

Marriage is like a hot bath.
Once you get used to it, it's not so hot.

Marriage is like a mousetrap. Those on the outside are trying to get in. Those on the inside are trying to get out.

Marriage is the process of finding out what kind of man your wife would have preferred.

Marriage: a ceremony in which rings are put on the finger of the lady and around the hands and feet of the man.

Marriage: the only sport in which the trapped animal has to buy the license

Marry not a tennis player. For love means nothing to them.

The days just before marriage are like a snappy introduction to a tedious book.

The only one of your children who does not grow up and move away is your husband.

The theory used to be you marry an older man because they are more mature. The new theory is that men don't mature. So you might as well marry a younger one.

All marriages are happy, it's the living together afterwards that causes all the problems.

Did you hear about the scientist whose wife had twins? He baptized one and kept the other as a control.

May you be blessed with a wife so healthy and strong, she can pull the plough when your horse drops dead.

May you learn to perform miracles:
earn a living and marry off your daughters.

A little boy, at a wedding looks at his mom and says, 'Mummy, why does the girl wear white?' His mother replies, 'The bride is in white because she's happy – this is the happiest day of her life.' The boy thinks about this, and then says, 'Well then, why is the boy wearing black?'

Married life is full of excitement and frustration:
In the first year of marriage, the man speaks
and the woman listens.
In the second year, the woman speaks and the man listens.
In the third year, they both speak and the neighbours listen.

A woman got on a bus holding a baby. The bus driver said: 'That's the ugliest baby I've ever seen.' In a huff, the woman slammed her fare into the fare box and took an aisle seat near the rear of the bus. The man seated next to her sensed that she was agitated and asked her what was wrong.
'The bus driver insulted me,' she fumed.
The man sympathized and said, 'Why, he's supposed to serve the public and be courteous and shouldn't say things to insult passengers.'
'You're right,' she said. 'I think I'll go back up there and give him a piece of my mind.'
'That's a good idea,' the man said.
'Here, let me hold your monkey.'

A guy in a bar notices a woman, always alone,
who comes in on a fairly regular basis.
After the second week, he made his move.
'No, thank you,' she said politely. 'This may sound
rather odd in this day and age, but I'm keeping myself
pure until I meet the man I love.'

'That must be rather difficult,' the man replied.
'Oh, I don't mind too much,' she said. 'But, it has my husband pretty upset.'

A small boy was lost, so he went up to a policeman and said, 'I've lost my dad!'
The copper said, 'What's he like?'
The little boy replied, 'Beer and women!'

A husband desperate to end an argument offers to buy his wife a new car. She curtly declines his offer by saying, 'That's not quite what I had in mind'.
Frantically he offers her a new house. Again she rejects his offer, 'That's not quite what I had in mind'.
Curious, he asks: 'What did you have in mind?'
She retorts, 'I'd like a divorce'.
He answers, 'I hadn't planned on spending quite that much'.

A convicted robber was given 10 years without parole for his latest crime. After two years in jail, he managed to escape.
His escape was the lead item on the six o'clock news.
Because he had to be careful, he worked his way home taking little-travelled routes, running across deserted fields and taking every precaution he could to outwit the search teams.
Eventually he arrived at his house and he rang the bell.
His wife opened the door and bellowed at him, 'You good-for-nothing! Where the hell have you been?
You escaped over six hours ago.'

A man was walking in the street when he heard a voice. 'Stop! Stand still! If you take one more step, a brick will fall down on your head and kill you.' The man stopped and a big brick fell right in front of him. The man was astonished. He went on, and after a while he was going to cross the

road. Once again the voice shouted: 'Stop! Stand still! If you take one more step a car will run over you and you will die.'
The man did as he was instructed, just as a car came careening around the corner, barely missing him.
'Where are you?' the man asked. 'Who are you?'
'I am your guardian angel,' the voice answered.
'Oh right!' the man asked. 'And where the hell were you when I got married?'

After the sermon was over, one member of the congregation had lingered after the other members and had shaken hands with the minister on his way out. The minister recognized the young man as one whom he had married a couple of months before. As the young man shook hands with the minister, he asked, 'Reverend, do you believe someone should profit from the mistakes of others?'
'Certainly not,' replied the preacher.
'Well, in that case, could I have the money back that I gave you for marrying me?'

Everybody on Earth dies and goes to heaven. God comes and says, 'I want the men to make two lines. Form one line for the men that dominated their women on Earth and another line for the men that were dominated by their women.
Also, I want all the women to go with St Peter.'
The next time God looks, the women are gone and there are two lines. The line of the men that were dominated by their women is 100 miles long, and in the line of men that dominated their women, there is only one man. God got angry and said, 'You men should be ashamed of yourselves. I created you in my image and you were dominated by your women. Look at the only one of my sons that stood up and made me proud. Learn from him! Tell them my son, how did you manage to be the only one in this line?' And the man replied, 'I don't know, my wife told me to stand here.'

I met a man who had been married for 66 years.
'Amazing. Sixty-six years!' I said. 'What's the secret to such a
long, happy marriage?'
'Well,' he replied, 'It's like this. The man makes all the big
decisions, and the woman just makes the little decisions.'
'Really?' I responded. 'Does that really work?'
'Oh, yes,' he said proudly. 'Sixty-six years, and so far,
not one big decision!'

A husband was just coming out of anaesthesia after having
surgery in the hospital, and his faithful wife was sitting at
his bedside. His eyes started to open and he quietly uttered,
'You're beautiful.'
He soon drifted back to sleep, and after awhile he woke up
and said, 'You're cute.'
'What happened to beautiful?' she asked him.
'The drugs are wearing off,' he replied.

The husband says to his wife, 'We really got to get rid of it. It's
old and smelly.'
She replies, 'Yes I know, it takes up a lot of room in the house
and it's scaring the kids.'
'So it's settled we're getting rid of it,' the husband says.
The wife nods her agreement, 'I think so'.
'Okay, I'll go get the car ready, you go get it.'
With this the wife goes to the foot of the stairs and yells,
'Grandad get ready – we're going for a drive!'

A young boy was looking through the family album
and asked his mother, 'Who's this guy on the beach with
you with all the muscles and curly hair?'
'That's your father.'
'Then who's that old bald-headed fat man
who lives with us now?'

A young woman entered a butcher's shop with a baby in her arms, and confronted the butcher with the news that the baby was his. Finally he offered to provide her with free meat until the boy was 16. She agreed. The butcher counted the years off on his calendar, and one day the teenager, who had been collecting the meat each week, came into the shop and said, 'I'll be sixteen tomorrow'.

'I know,' said the butcher with a smile, 'I've been counting too. Tell your mother when you take this parcel of meat home, that it is the last free meat she'll get, and watch the expression on her face.'

When the boy arrived home he told his mother. The woman nodded and said, 'Son, go back to the butcher and tell him I have also had free bread, free milk, and free groceries for the last sixteen years and watch the expression on his face!'

Mary's three children were driving her insane. She complained to her best friend, 'They're driving me mad. Such pests, they give me no rest and I'm halfway to the lunatic asylum.'

'What you need is a playpen to separate the kids from yourself,' her friend said. So Mary bought a playpen. A few days later, her friend called to ask how things were going. 'Superb! I can't believe it,' Mary said. 'I get in that pen with a good book and the kids don't bother me one bit!'

A woman takes her 16-year-old daughter to the doctor. The doctor says, 'Yes, Mrs Jones, what seems to be the problem?' The mother says, 'It's my daughter Julie. She keeps getting these cravings, she's putting on weight, and is sick most mornings.' The doctor gives Julie a good examination, then turns to the mother and says, 'Well, I don't know how to tell you this, but your Julie is pregnant – about four months would be my guess.' The mother says, 'Pregnant? She can't be, she has never ever been left alone with a man! Have you, Julie?' Julie says, 'No mother! I've never even kissed a man!' The doctor walks over to the window and just stares out of it. About five minutes pass and finally the mother says, 'Is there something wrong out there doctor?' The doctor replies, 'No, not really, it's just that the last time anything like this happened, a star appeared in the east and three wise men came over the hill.'

A man is walking down the beach and comes across an old bottle. He picks it up, pulls out the cork and out pops a genie. The genie says 'Thank you for freeing me from the bottle. In return I will grant you three wishes.' The man says 'Great. I always dreamed of this and I know exactly what I want. First, I want a billion pounds in a Swiss bank account.' Poof! There is a flash of light and a piece of paper with account numbers appears in his hand. He continues, 'Next, I want a brand new red Ferrari right here'. Poof! There is a flash of light and a bright red brand-new Ferrari appears right next to him. He continues, 'Finally, I want to be irresistible to women.'. Poof! There is a flash of light and he turns into a box of chocolates.

Eight-year-old Sally brought her report card home from school.
Her marks were very good, mostly As and a couple of Bs.
However, her teacher had written across the bottom: 'Sally is a
clever little girl, but she has one fault. She talks too much in
school. I have an idea I am going to try, which I think may
break her of the habit.'
Sally's dad signed her report card, putting a note on the back:
'Please let me know if your idea works on Sally because I would
like to try it out on her mother.'

**A wife woke of the middle of the night to find her husband
missing from bed. She got out of bed and checked around
the house. She heard sobbing from the basement.
After turning on the light and descending the stairs, she
found her husband curled up into a little ball, sobbing.
'Darling, what's wrong?' she asked, worried about what
could hurt him so much.
'Remember, twenty years ago, I got you pregnant? And your
father threatened me to marry you or to go to jail?'
'Yes, of course,' she replied.
'Well, I would have been released tonight.'**

Why would you ever want to remarry an ex-spouse?
It's like finding some sour milk, putting it in the rubbish bin for
a couple of days, and then wondering to yourself: 'Well, I
wonder if it'll taste any better now.'

**At a cocktail party, one woman said to another, 'Aren't you
wearing your wedding ring on the wrong finger?'
The other replied, 'Yes I am – I married the wrong man.'**

'Mr Smith, I have reviewed this case very carefully,'
the divorce court judge said, 'and I've decided to
give your wife money every week.'

'That's very nice, your honour,' the husband said. 'And every now and then I'll try to send her a few pounds, myself.'

Tony's wife bought a new line of expensive cosmetics guaranteed to make her look years younger. After a lengthy sitting before the mirror applying the 'miracle' products she asked, 'Darling, honestly what age would you say I am?'
Looking over her carefully, Tony replied, 'Judging from your skin, twenty; your hair, eighteen; and your figure, twenty-five.'
'Oh, you flatterer!' she gushed.
'Hey, wait a minute!' Tony interrupted. 'I haven't added them up yet.'

The last fight we had was my fault. My wife asked,
'What's on the TV?'
I said, 'Dust!'

In the beginning God created Earth and rested. Then God created man and rested. Then God decided to create woman. Since then neither God nor man has rested.

My wife and I are inseparable.
In fact, last week it took four policemen and a dog.

Do you know the punishment for bigamy?
Two mothers-in-law.

The most effective way to remember your wife's birthday is to forget it once.

How do most men define marriage?
It's an expensive way to get their washing done for free.

I never knew what real happiness was until I got married;
then it was too late.

Women will never be equal to men until they can walk down the street with a bald head and a beer gut, and still think they look beautiful.

DO I LOOK FAT?

The correct male response to this question is to confidently and emphatically state, 'No, of course not' and then quickly leave the room. Wrong answers include:

'I wouldn't call you fat, but I wouldn't call you thin either.'

'Compared to what?'

'A little extra weight looks good on you.'

'I've seen fatter.'

'Could you repeat the question, I need more time to consider my answer.'

DO YOU THINK SHE'S PRETTIER THAN ME?

The 'she' in the question could be an ex-girlfriend, a passer-by you were staring at so hard that you almost cause a traffic accident or an actress in a film you just saw. In any case, the correct response is, 'No, you are much prettier.' Wrong answers include:

'Not prettier, just pretty in a different way.'

'I don't know how one goes about rating such things.'

'Yes, but I bet you have a better personality.'

'Only in the sense that she's younger and thinner.'

'Could you repeat the question?'

DO YOU LOVE ME?

The correct answer to this question is, 'Yes'. For those guys who feel the need to be more elaborate, you may answer, 'Yes, dear.' Wrong answers include:

'I suppose so.'

'Would it make you feel better if I said yes.'

'That depends on what you mean by "love".'

'Does it matter?'

A man was walking along the sea front in Dover when he found a bottle. He looked around and didn't see anyone so he opened it. A genie appeared and thanked the man for letting him out. The genie said, 'For your kindness I will grant you one wish, but only one.' The man thought for a minute and said, 'I have always wanted to go to France but have never been able to because I'm afraid of flying and ships make me claustrophobic and ill. So, I wish for a bridge to be built from here to France.'
The genie thought for a few minutes and said, 'No, I don't think I can do that. Just think of all the work involved with the pilings needed to hold up the road and how deep they would have to be to reach the bottom of the sea.'
'No, that is just too much to ask,' replied the man.
The man thought for a minute and then told the genie, 'There is one other thing that I have always wanted. I would like to be able to understand women. What makes them laugh and cry, why are they temperamental, why are they so difficult to get along with? Basically, what makes them tick?'
The genie considered for a few minutes and said, 'So, do you want two lanes or four?'

A woman worries about the future until she gets a husband. A man never worries about the future until he gets a wife.

A successful man is one who makes more money that his wife can spend.
A successful woman is one who can find such a man.

Any married man should forget his mistakes – there's no use in two people remembering the same thing.

A woman has the last word in any argument. Anything a man says after that is the beginning of a new argument.

Mary was having a tough day and had stretched herself out on the sofa to do a bit of what she thought to be well-deserved complaining and self- pitying. She moaned to her mum and brother, 'Nobody loves me ... the whole world hates me!' Her brother, busily occupied playing a game, hardly looked up at her and passed on this encouraging word: 'That's not true, Mary. Some people don't even know you.'

An old man was walking on the beach with his only grandson, when a giant wave crashes on shore, sweeping the boy out to sea. The man looks up to the heavens and says: 'Oh Lord, this is my only grandson. How can you take him away from me like this? My son will not understand. My daughter-in-law will die from grief.' Another wave comes by, and deposits the boy at the old man's feet. The grandfather looks to the heavens again and says, 'He had a hat!'

At a jewellery store, a young man bought an expensive locket as a present for his girlfriend. 'Don't you want her name engraved upon it?' asked the jeweller. The young man thought for a moment, and then, ever the pragmatic, steadfastly replied, 'No, just engrave it: To My One And Only Love. That way, if we break up and she throws it back to me in anger, I can use it again.'

An absent-minded husband thought he had conquered the problem of trying to remember his wife's birthday and their anniversary. He opened an account with a florist, provided that florist with the dates and instructions to send flowers to his wife on these dates along with an appropriate note signed, 'Your loving husband'. His wife was thrilled by this new display of attention and all went well until one day, some bouquets later, when he came

home, kissed his wife and said in an offhand manner,
'Nice flowers, darling. Where'd you get them?'

'I'm ashamed of you,' the mother said. 'Fighting with your best
friend is a terrible thing to do!'
'He threw a rock at me!' the boy said. 'So I threw one at him.'
The mother stated emphatically, 'When he threw a rock at
you, you should have come to me.'
The boy quickly replied, 'What good would that have done?
My aim is much better than yours.'

**A man's wife had been killed in an accident
and the police were questioning him.
'Did she say anything before she died?' asked the sergeant.
'She spoke without interruption for about forty years,'
replied the husband.**

A man was talking to his GP and said, 'Doc, I'm afraid you'll
have to remove my wife's tonsils one of these days.'
The doctor pulled out the family's medical file and exclaimed,
'Why, I removed them six years ago! Did you ever hear of a
woman having two sets of tonsils?'
'No,' the husband retorted. 'But you've heard
of a man having two wives, haven't you?'

**One March day my wife said that the house needed
painting. 'It's still winter,' I replied. 'Forget it.'
In April, she told me she had bought some exterior paint.
I said that it was still too cold to paint. In May, I heard her
outside one day yelling for help, and we set up the ladder so
she could start painting. Then I went inside to get a beer.
As I sat in a lawn chair not far from where my wife was
working, a neighbour passed by.
'Aren't you ashamed?' she asked. 'How can you sit there**

drinking beer while your wife is up on a
ladder painting the house?'
Glancing up at my wife, I responded, 'She doesn't like beer.'

John decides to paint the toilet seat one morning while his wife
is away. The job done, he heads to the kitchen to raid the
refrigerator. Mary, his wife, comes home sooner than expected,
and, needing to visit the toilet, sits down and gets the toilet
seat stuck to her rear. In a panic, Mary shouts for John to drive
her to the doctor. She puts on a large overcoat to cover the
stuck seat, and off they go.
When they get to the doctor's office, John lifts his wife's coat to
show their predicament. John asks, 'Doctor, have you ever seen
anything like this before?'
'Well, yes,' the doctor admits. 'But never framed.'

Billy was now old enough to take a driving test. He passed
first time and his licence dropped through the letter box
several days later. To celebrate, the whole family trooped out
and climbed into the car for his inaugural drive.
Dad immediately headed to the back seat, directly behind
the new driver.
'I'll bet you're back there to get a change of scenery after all
those months of sitting in the front passenger seat teaching
me how to drive,' said the beaming boy to his father.
'No,' came Dad's reply, 'I'm going to sit here and kick the
back of your seat as you drive, just like you've been doing to
me for sixteen years.'

One summer evening during a violent thunderstorm a mother
was tucking her son into bed. She was about to turn off the
light when he asked with a tremor in his voice, 'Mummy, will
you sleep with me tonight?'
The mother smiled and gave him a reassuring hug. 'I can't
dear,' she said. 'I have to sleep in Daddy's room.'

A long silence was broken at last by his shaky little voice:
'The big sissy.'

It was that time, during the Sunday morning service, for the
children's sermon. All the children were invited to come
forward. One little girl was wearing a particularly pretty
dress and, as she sat down, the vicar leaned over and said,
'That is a very pretty dress. Is it your Easter dress?'
The little girl replied, directly into the pastor's clip-on
microphone, 'Yes, and my Mum says it's a bitch to iron.'

An exasperated mother, whose son was always getting into
mischief, finally asked him, 'How do you expect to get into
Heaven?' The boy thought it over and said, 'Well, I'll run in
and out and in an out and keep slamming the door until St
Peter says, 'For Heaven's sake Dylan, come in or stay out!'

When I was six months pregnant with my
third child, my three-year-old came into
the room just as I was just getting
ready to get into the shower.
She said, 'Mummy, you are getting fat!'
I replied, 'Yes, darling, remember
Mummy has a baby growing in
her tummy.'
'I know,' she replied, but
what's growing in your bum?'

Linda, a radical feminist, is
getting on a bus to go to work.
As she walks down the aisle to
find a seat a man just in front of
her gets up. Linda thinks to herself,
'Here's another man trying to keep up

the customs of a male-dominated society by offering a poor, defenceless woman his seat,' and so she pushes him back on to the seat. A few minutes later, the man tries to get up again. Linda is further insulted and refuses to let him up. Finally, the flabbergasted man says, 'Look, you've got to let me get up. I'm two miles past my stop already!'

How many men does it take to open a beer?
None. It should be opened by the time she brings it.

Why is a launderette a really bad place to pick up a woman? Because a woman who can't even afford a washing machine will probably never be able to support you.

If your dog is barking at the back door and your wife is yelling at the front door, whom do you let in first?
The dog of course. He'll shut up once you let him in.

What's worse than a Male Chauvinist Pig?
A woman who won't do what she's told.

I married Miss Right.
I just didn't know her first name was Always.

Scientists have discovered a food that diminishes a woman's sex drive by 90 per cent. It's called a Wedding Cake.

'OLD' IS WHEN... Your spouse says, 'Let's go upstairs and make love,' and you answer, 'Pick one, I can't do both!'

'OLD' IS WHEN... Your friends compliment you on your new crocodile shoes and you're barefoot.

'OLD' IS WHEN... A good-looking woman catches your fancy and your pacemaker opens the garage door.

'OLD' IS WHEN... Going bra-less pulls all the wrinkles out of your face.

'OLD' IS WHEN... You don't care where your spouse goes, just as long as you don't have to go along.

'OLD' IS WHEN... You are cautioned to slow down by the doctor instead of by the police.

'OLD' IS WHEN... 'Getting a little action' means I don't need to take any fibre today.

'OLD' IS WHEN... 'Getting lucky' means you find your car in the parking lot.

'OLD' IS WHEN... An 'all-nighter' means not getting up to pee.

A man asked his wife, 'What would you most like for your birthday?' She said, 'I'd love to be ten again.' On the morning of her birthday, he got her up bright and early and they went to a theme park. He put her on every ride in the park – the Death Slide, The Screaming Loop, the Wall of Fear. She had a go on every ride there was. She staggered out of the theme park five hours later, her head reeling and her stomach turning. Then they went off to a see a film, popcorn, cola and sweets. At last she staggered home with her husband and collapsed into bed. Her husband leaned over and asked, 'Well, dear, what was it like being ten again?' One eye opened and she groaned, 'Actually, darling, I meant dress size!'

A man placed some flowers on the grave of his dearly departed mother and started back toward his car when his attention was diverted to another man kneeling at a grave.

The man seemed to be praying with profound intensity and kept repeating, 'Why did you have to die? Why did you have to die? Why did you have to die?'
The first man approached him and said, 'Sir, I don't wish to interfere with your private grief, but this demonstration of pain is more than I've ever seen before. For whom do you mourn so deeply? A child? A parent?'
The mourner took a moment to collect his thoughts then replied, 'My wife's first husband'.

After being away on business, Tim thought it would be nice to bring his wife a little gift. 'How about some perfume?' he asked the cosmetics assistant. She showed him an expensive bottle. 'That's a bit much,' said Tim, so she returned with a smaller bottle for slightly less. 'That's still quite a bit,' Tim complained. Growing annoyed, the assistant brought out a tiny bottle. 'What I mean,' said Tim, 'is I'd like to see something really cheap.' The assistant handed him a mirror.

Men are like photocopiers.
You need them for reproduction, but that's about it.

Men are like high heels. They're easy to walk on once you get the hang of it.

Men are like curling irons. They're always hot, and they're always in your hair.

Men are like mini skirts. If you're not careful, they'll creep up your legs.

I haven't spoken to my wife for 18 months.
I don't like to interrupt her.

A man inserted an advertisement in the classifieds section with the heading 'Wife Wanted'. The next day he received 100 letters saying, 'You can have mine.'

A teacher's pupils were leaving her class for the last time and every one of them brought her a present.
The florist's son handed her a gift. She shook it, held it over her head, and said, 'I bet I know what it is – flowers!'
'That's right!' said the boy, 'but how did you know?'
'Just a wild guess,' she said.
The next pupil was the sweet-shop owner's daughter.
The teacher held her gift overhead, shook it, and said, 'I bet I can guess what it is – a box of chocolates!'
'That's right! But how did you know?' asked the girl.
'Just a lucky guess,' said the teacher.
The next gift was from the off-license owner's son. The teacher held the bag over her head and noticed that it was leaking. She touched a drop of the leakage with her finger and tasted it. 'Is it wine?' she asked. 'No,' the boy replied.
The teacher repeated the process, touching another drop of the leakage to her tongue. 'Is it champagne?' she asked.
'No,' the boy replied. The teacher then said, 'I give up, what is it?' The boy replied, 'A puppy!'

Johnny's mother asked him what he had learned in Sunday school. 'Well, mum, our teacher told us how God sent Moses behind enemy lines on a rescue mission to lead the Israelites out of Egypt. When he got to the Red Sea he had his engineers build a pontoon bridge and all the people walked across safely.
Then he used his walkie-talkie to radio headquarters for reinforcements. They sent bombers to blow up the bridge and saved the Israelites.'
'Now, Johnny, is that really what your teacher taught you?' his mother asked.

'Well, no, mum, but if I told it the way the teacher did, you'd never believe it.'

TODDLER'S DIET PLAN: DAY ONE

Breakfast – One scrambled egg, one piece of toast with jam. Eat two bites of egg using your fingers; dump the rest on the floor. Take one bite of toast, and then smear the jam over your face and clothes.
Lunch – Four crayons (any colour), a handful of crisps, and a glass of milk – three sips, then spill the rest.
Dinner – A dry stick, two coins, four sips of flat diet cola.
Bedtime snack – Toast a piece of bread, butter it, and toss it face down on the floor.

TODDLER'S DIET PLAN: DAY TWO

Breakfast – Pick up stale toast from the floor and eat it. Drink 1/2 bottle of vanilla extract or small bottle of vegetable dye.
Lunch – Half a tube of lipstick and one ice cube, if desired.
Afternoon snack – Dummy until sticky, take it outside and drop in dirt. Retrieve and continue slurping until clean again, then bring inside and drop on living room carpet.
Dinner – A stone or an uncooked bean, which should then be thrust up your left nostril. Pour iced tea over mashed potatoes, eat with spoon.

TODDLER'S DIET PLAN: DAY THREE

Breakfast – Two pancakes with plenty of syrup eat with fingers; rub fingers in hair to clean. Glass of milk, drink half, stuff excess pancakes in glass. After breakfast, pick up yesterday's dummy from carpet, lick off fuzz until sticky again, then leave on cushion of your best chair.
Lunch – Peanut butter and jam sandwich. Spit several well-chewed bites on to the floor. Pour glass of milk on to table, and then slurp up.
Dinner – Dish of ice cream, handful of crisps.

TODDLER'S DIET PLAN: LAST DAY
Breakfast – 1/4 tube of toothpaste (any flavour), bite of soap
and one olive. Pour glass of milk over bowl of cornflakes, add
1/2 cup of sugar. Wait until cereal is soggy, drink milk and
feed cereal to dog with your spoon.
Lunch – Eat crumbs off the kitchen floor and
dining-room carpet.
Dinner – A plate of spaghetti and chocolate milkshake.
Leave meatball on plate. Handful of cheese snacks, eat two
and place the rest in convenient hiding place.

THINGS I'VE LEARNED FROM MY CHILDREN

There is no such thing as childproofing your house.
A four-year-old's voice is louder than 200 adults in a crowded restaurant.
If you hook a dog lead over a ceiling fan the motor is not strong enough to rotate a 42 lb boy wearing underwear and a superman cape.
Tennis balls make marks on ceilings

MORE THINGS I'VE LEARNED FROM MY CHILDREN
When you hear a toilet flush and the words 'Uh-oh', it's
already too late.
**A six-year-old boy can start a fire with a flint even though a
36-year-old man says they can only do that in the movies.**
A magnifying glass can start a fire even on an overcast day.
A king-size waterbed holds enough water to fill a 2,000

square foot house three inches deep.
Lego will pass through the digestive track of a four-year-old.
Duplo will not.

EVEN MORE THINGS I'VE LEARNED
FROM MY CHILDREN
**Play dough and microwave should never
be used in the same sentence.**
Super glue is forever.
Marbles in petrol tanks make lots of noise when driving.
You probably don't want to know what that smell is.

FINAL THINGS I'VE LEARNED FROM MY CHILDREN
Always look in the oven before you turn it on.
Plastic toys do not like ovens.
Cats throw up twice their body weight when dizzy.
Quiet does not necessarily mean don't worry.
A good sense of humour will get you through most problems in
life (unfortunately, mostly in retrospect).

A clergyman was walking down the street when he came
upon a group of about a dozen boys, all of them between 10
and 12 years of age. The group surrounded a dog.
Concerned that the boys were hurting the dog, he went over
and asked 'What are you doing with that dog?' One of the
boys replied, 'This dog is just an old stray. We all want him,
but only one of us can take him home. So we've decided
that whichever one of us can tell the biggest lie will get to
keep the dog.'
'You boys shouldn't be having a contest telling lies!' the
clergyman exclaimed. He then launched into a 10-minute
sermon against lying, beginning, 'Don't you boys know it's a
sin to lie,' and ending with, 'Why, when I was your age, I
never told a lie.' There was dead silence for about a minute.
Just as the clergyman was beginning to think he'd got

through to them, the smallest boy gave a deep sigh and said, 'All right, give him the dog.'

A Sunday school teacher was teaching her class about the difference between right and wrong.
'All right children, let's take another example,' she said. 'If I were to get into a man's pocket and take his wallet with all his money, what would I be?'
Little Johnny raised his hand, and with a confident smile, he blurted out, 'You'd be his wife!'

On the first day of school, about mid-morning, the kindergarten teacher said, 'If anyone has to go to the bathroom, hold up two fingers.' A little voice from the back of the room asked, 'How will that help?'

Women have many faults, men only have two.
Everything they say and everything they do.

Love is one long sweet dream. Marriage is the alarm clock.

LOVE – When your eyes meet across a crowded room.
LUST – When your tongues meet across a crowded room.
MARRIAGE – When your belt won't meet around your waist, and you don't care.
LOVE – When you write poems about your partner.
LUST – When all you write is your phone number.
MARRIAGE – When all you write is cheques.
LOVE – When you are proud to be seen in public with your partner.
LUST – When you only ever see each other in the bedroom.
MARRIAGE – When you never see each other awake.
LOVE – When nobody else matters.
LUST – When nobody else knows.

MARRIAGE – When everybody else matters and you don't care who knows.

LOVE – When all the songs on the radio describe exactly how you feel.

LUST – When it's just the same mushy old rubbish.

MARRIAGE – When you never listen to music.

LOVE – When breaking up is something you try not to think about.

LUST – When staying together is something you try not to think about.

MARRIAGE – When just getting through today is your only thought.

LOVE – When you're interested in everything your partner does.

LUST – When you're only interested in one thing.

MARRIAGE – When you're not interested in what your partner does and the one thing you're interested in is the football scores.

They say when a man holds a woman's hand before marriage, it is love; after marriage, it is self-defence.

If Yoko Ono married Sonny Bono, she'd be Yoko Ono Bono.

If Dolly Parton married Salvador Dali, she'd be Dolly Dali.

If Sondra Locke married Elliott Ness, and then divorced him to marry Herman Munster, she'd become Sondra Locke Ness Munster.

If Ivana Trump married, in succession, Orson Bean (actor), King Oscar (of Norway), Louis B. Mayer (of MGM), and Norbert Wiener (mathematician), she would then be Ivana Bean Oscar Mayer Wiener.

If Woody Allen married Natalie Wood, divorced her and married Gregory Peck, divorced him and married Ben Hur, he'd be Woody Wood Peck Hur.

Bottle-feeding is an opportunity for the father to get up at 2 a.m. too.

Family planning is the art of spacing your children the proper distance apart to keep you on the edge of financial disaster.

Feedback is the inevitable result when the baby doesn't appreciate the strained carrots.

A full name is what you call your child when you're mad at him.

Grandparents are people who think your children are wonderful even though they're sure you're not raising them right.

Hearsay is what toddlers do when anyone mutters a dirty word.

Prenatal is when your life was still somewhat your own.

Sterilizing is what you do to your first baby's dummy by boiling it, and to your last baby's dummy by blowing on it.

Temper tantrums are what you should keep to a minimum so as to not upset the children.

Little Johnny's father said, 'let me see your report card.'
Johnny replied, 'I don't have it.'
'Why not?' His father asked.
'My friend just borrowed it. He wants to scare his parents.'

Little Johnny was sitting on a park bench munching on one chocolate bar after another. After the sixth one a man on the bench across from him said, 'Son, you know eating all that sweets aren't good for you. It will give you acne, rot your teeth, make you fat.' Little Johnny replied, 'My grandfather lived to be 107 years old.' The man asked, 'Did your grandfather eat six chocolate bars at a time?' Little Johnny answered, 'No, he minded his own business!'

At Sunday school they were teaching how God created everything, including human beings. Little Johnny seemed especially interested when they told him how Eve was created out of one of Adam's ribs.
Later in the week his mother noticed him lying down as though he were ill, and said, 'Johnny what is the matter?' Little Johnny responded, 'I have a pain in my side. I think I'm going to have a wife.'

Coming through the door after school one day, Little Johnny shouts out: 'Okay everyone in the house, please stand advised that I, Little Johnny, have on this date made a complete fool of myself in sex-education class by repeating stories concerning storks as told to me by certain parties residing in this house!'

Little Johnny watched, fascinated, as his mother gently rubbed cold cream on her face. 'Why are you rubbing cold cream on your face, Mummy?' he asked.
'To make myself beautiful,' said his mother.
A few minutes later, she began removing the cream with a tissue. 'What's the matter?' asked Little Johnny. 'Giving up?'

Little Johnny's neighbour has just had a little boy. The only problem is that the baby doesn't have any ears. Everyone who comes to see the baby compliments the woman on its

looks, but no one mentions the fact that it
doesn't have any ears.
Suddenly, the mother sees Little Johnny coming over from
next door. She becomes very worried because she thinks
that he is going to make fun of the baby.
When he enters the house, he compliments the baby on
everything without mentioning its ears. Without warning,
he says, 'He has beautiful eyes, does he have 20/20 vision?'
So she thanks him and asks why.
Finally he says, 'Well, it's a good thing because if he didn't,
he wouldn't have anything to hang his glasses on
now would he?'

Two parents were discussing a man who was running for
parliament. 'He's a Falkland's War veteran,' commented the
husband. 'What's that?' queried their young daughter. Trying
to answer the question in terms a four-year-old could readily
grasp, the husband replied, 'Well, that means that the man
fought in a war that happened when Mummy and Daddy were
little.' The daughter regarded them both thoughtfully for a
moment, and then asked, 'So, was he a Viking?'

Wilfred had just learned his alphabet and was very scared of
recited it in front of the class. The teacher told him that the
best way to conquer his fears would be to just go ahead and
do it. So, trembling, he stood in front of the class and began.
'ABCDEFGHIJLKMNOQRSTUVWXYZ.'
'Very good, Wilfred. But you forgot the P. Where's the P?
'It's running down my leg.'

A man escaped from prison by digging a hole from his cell to
the outside world. When finally his work was done, he emerged
in the middle of a infant school playground.
'I'm free, I'm free!' he shouted.
'So what,' said a little girl. 'I'm four.'

If you are thinking of having children, think again.
Try this mess test:
Smear peanut butter on the sofa and curtains. Now rub your hands in the wet flowerbed and rub on the walls. Cover the stains with crayons. Place a fish finger behind the couch and leave it there all summer.

If you are thinking of having children, think again.
Try this toy test:
Obtain a 55-gallon box of Lego. (If Lego is not available, you may substitute roofing tacks or broken bottles.) Have a friend spread them all over the house. Put on a blindfold. Try to walk to the toilet or kitchen. Do not scream (this could wake a child at night).

If you are thinking of having children, think again.
Try this supermarket test:
Borrow one or two small animals (goats are best) and take them with you as you shop at the supermarket. Always keep them in sight and pay for anything they eat or damage.

If you are thinking of having children, think again.
Try this getting dressed test:
Obtain one large, unhappy, live octopus. Try to stuff into a small net bag, making sure that all arms stay inside.

If you are thinking of having children, think again.
Try this feeding test:
Obtain a large plastic milk jug. Fill halfway with water. Suspend from the ceiling with a stout cord. Start the jug swinging. Try to insert spoonfuls of soggy cereal into the mouth of the jug while pretending to be a train. Now dump the contents of the jug on the floor.

A little girl was failing maths. Her mother enrolled her in Catholic school in the hopes to improve her maths grades. During the first marking period, her mother noticed a dramatic improvement in her math studies. The girl would refuse to play with friends or to eat dessert after dinner in order to study more. On report card day, her mother was astonished to see that her daughter got an A+ in maths. She asked her daughter, 'Why the sudden change of attitude about maths? Do the nuns punish you?'
The girl replied, 'No, but when I saw the little man on the wall nailed to the plus sign, I knew that this school is very serious about maths!'

A pregnant woman is in a car accident and falls into a deep coma. Asleep for nearly six months, she wakes up and sees that she is no longer pregnant. Frantically, she asks the doctor about her baby. The doctor replies, 'You had twins! You had a boy and a girl. The babies are fine. Your brother came in and named them.'
The woman thinks to herself, 'Oh no, not my brother, he's an idiot!' Expecting the worst, she asks the doctor, 'Well, what's the girl's name?'
'Denise,' the doctor says.
The new mother thinks, 'Wow, that's not a bad name! Guess I was wrong about my brother. I like Denise!'
Then she asks the doctor, 'What's the boy's name?'
The doctor replies, 'Denephew'.

A boy was at a public swimming pool.
The lifeguard blew his whistle at the boy and yelled, 'Hey! Don't pee in the pool!'
The boy replied, 'But everybody does it!'
'Not from the diving board!' shouted the lifeguard.

A primary school teacher asks her class to make up a sentence with the word 'fascinate' in it. A little girl stands up and says, 'Elephants are so fascinating.'
The teacher says, 'No, that's not correct. I said, fascinate.'
Another little girl stands up and says, 'There's so much fascination when it comes to sea life.'
The teacher again says, 'No, the word is fascinate.'
So a little boy in the back of the room stands up and says, 'Well, my sister has such a big stomach that she can only fascinate of the ten buttons on her shirt.'

A little girl is sitting on her grandpa's lap and studying the wrinkles on his old face. She gets up the nerve to rub her fingers over the wrinkles. Then she touches her own face and looks more puzzled. Finally the little girl asks, 'Grandpa, did God make you?'
'Of course he did, a long time ago,' replies her Grandpa.
'Well, did God make me?' asks the little girl.
'Yes, He did, and that wasn't too long ago,' answers her Grandpa. 'Well,' says the little girl, 'He's doing a lot better job these days isn't He?'

At school, a boy is told by a classmate that most adults are hiding at least one dark secret, and that this makes it very easy to blackmail them by saying, 'I know the whole truth', even when you don't know anything.
The boy decides to go home and try it out. As he is greeted by his mother at the front door he says, 'I know the whole truth'. His mother quickly

hands him some money and says, 'Just don't tell your father.' Quite pleased, the boy waits for his father to get home from work, and greets him with, 'I know the whole truth'. The father promptly hands him some money and says, 'Please don't say a word to your mother'. Very pleased, the boy is on his way to school the next day, when he sees the milkman at his front door. The boy greets him by saying, 'I know the whole truth.'
The milkman drops the crate of milk, opens his arms and says, 'Then come give your father a big hug'.

One day, the phone rang, and a little boy answered.
'May I speak to your parents?'
'They're busy.'
'Oh. Is anybody else there?'
'The police.'
'Can I speak to them?'
'They're busy.'
'Oh. Is anybody else there?'
'The firemen.'
'Can I speak to them?'
'They're busy.'
'So let me get this straight. Your parents, the police, and the firemen are there, but they're all busy? What are they doing?'
'Looking for me.'

THINGS CHILDREN LEARN
No matter how hard you try, you can't baptize cats.
When your mother is mad at your dad, don't let her brush your hair.
If your sister hits you, don't hit her back. They always catch the second person.
Never ask your three-year-old brother to hold a tomato.
You can't trust dogs to watch your food.

MORE THINGS CHILDREN LEARN
Reading what people write on desks can teach you a lot.
Don't sneeze when someone is cutting your hair.
Never hold a vacuum cleaner and a cat at the same time.
School lunches stick to the wall.
You can't hide a piece of broccoli in a glass of milk.

Billy, aged four, came screaming out of the bathroom to tell his father he'd dropped his toothbrush in the toilet. So his father fished it out and threw it in the rubbish bin.
Billy stood there thinking for a moment, then ran to the bathroom and came out with his father's toothbrush. He held it up and said with a charming little smile, 'We better throw this one out too then, because it fell in the toilet a few days ago.'

There were three boys at the zoo and the zookeeper
came up to them and asked for their names and
what they were trying to do.
The first boy said, 'My name is Tommy and I was trying to feed
peanuts to the lions'.
The second boy said, 'My name is Billy and I was trying to feed
peanuts to the lions'.
The third boy said, 'My name is Peanuts'.

What do you call a woman who has lost 95 per cent of her intelligence?
Divorced.

'I just got a new set of golf clubs for my wife!'
'Great trade!'

Little Johnny's dad picked him up from school. Knowing the parts for the school play were supposed to be posted today, he asked his son if he got a part.

Little Johnny enthusiastically announced that he had got a part. 'I play a man who's been married for twenty years.' 'That's great, son. Keep up the good work and before you know it they'll be giving you a speaking part.'

A Sunday school teacher was discussing the Ten Commandments with her young class. After explaining the commandment 'Honour thy father and thy mother', she asked 'Is there a commandment that teaches us how to treat our brothers and sisters?' Without missing a beat Little Johnny answered, 'Thou shall not kill'.

Teacher: 'If I had seven oranges in one hand and eight oranges in the other, what would I have?' Little Johnny: 'Big hands!'

During an English lesson, the teacher asked the students, 'Now tell me. What do you call a person who keeps on talking when people are no longer interested?' Little Johnny, at the back of the class replied, 'A teacher'.

Little Johnny said to his Aunt Betty, 'My God, you're ugly, aren't you!' His mother overheard this and pulled Johnny into the kitchen.'You naughty boy!' she screamed, 'How can you say to your aunt that she's ugly! You go right in and apologize to her! Tell her you're sorry!' Little Johnny entered the living room, walked over to his aunt and said, 'Aunt Betty, I am sorry you're so ugly.'

A teacher spent the entire hour reading to her class about the rhinoceros family. When she had finished, she said, 'Name some things that are very dangerous to get near to and have horns.' Little Johnny spoke up without hesitation, 'Cars!'

**Little Johnny asks a pregnant woman:
'What is in your tummy?'
'My baby!'
'Do you love him!'
'Of course I do!'
'Why did you eat him then?'**

A father is in church with his young children, including his
five-year-old son, Little Johnny.
During this particular service, the vicar was performing the
baptism of a tiny infant. Little Johnny was taken by this,
observing that he was saying something and pouring water
over the infant's head.
With a quizzical look on his face, Little Johnny turned to his
father and asked, 'Daddy, why is he brainwashing that baby?'

**'Mummy, Mummy', said Little Johnny one day, 'do you
know the beautiful vase in the dining room that's been
handed down from generation to generation?'
'Yes', said his mother. 'What about it?'
'Well, the last generation just dropped it.'**

Little Johnny was a bit of a tearaway. His mother suggested to
his father that they buy him a bike for his birthday.
'Do you really believe that'll help improve his behaviour?' he
said, surprised.
'Well, no,' she admitted, 'But it'll spread it over a wider area.'

**Teacher: 'Where were you born?'
Little Johnny: 'London.'
Teacher: 'Which part?'
Little Johnny: 'All of me.'**

Little Johnny and his friend were always boasting of their
parents achievements to each other.

Friend: 'Have you ever heard of the Suez Canal?'
Little Johnny: 'Yes, I have'
Friend: 'Well, my father dug it.'
Little Johnny: 'That's nothing, have you ever heard of the
Dead Sea?'
Friend: 'Yes, I have.'
Little Johnny: 'Well, my father killed it.'

**Little Johnny, eight years old, had never spoken a word.
One afternoon, as he sat eating his lunch he turned to his
mother and said, 'Soup's cold'.
His astonished mother exclaimed, 'Johnny, I've waited so
long to hear you speak. But all these years you never said a
thing. Why haven't you spoken before?'
Little Johnny looked at her and replied, 'Up until now,
everything's been okay'.**

Three boys are in the schoolyard bragging about their fathers.
The first boy says, 'My Dad scribbles a few words on a piece of
paper, he calls it a poem, they give him £50.'
The second boy says, 'That's nothing. My Dad
scribbles a few words on a piece of paper, he calls it a song,
and they give him £100.'
Little Johnny says, 'I got you both beat. My Dad scribbles a few
words on a piece of paper, he calls it a sermon and it takes
eight people to collect all the money!'

**Little Johnny greeted his grandmother with a hug and said,
'I'm so happy to see you Grandma. Now maybe Daddy will
do the trick he has been promising us.'
The grandmother was curious. 'What trick is that
my dear,' she asked.
Little Johnny replied, 'I heard Daddy tell Mummy that he
would climb up the wall if you came to visit us again.'**

Little Johnny sat playing in the garden. When his mother came out to collect him, she saw that he was slowly eating a worm. She turned pale. 'No, Johnny! Stop! That's horrible! You can't eat worms!'
Trying to convince him further, 'Now the mother worm is looking all over for her nice baby-worm.'
'No, she isn't,' said Little Johnny.
'Why not?' said the mother.
'I ate her first!'

A teacher asked her students if they could use the words 'defeat, defence and detail' in a sentence. Little Johnny answered with, 'De feet of de dog went over de fence before de tail.'

'Little Johnny, where's your homework?' Miss Martin said sternly to the little boy while holding out her hand.
'My dog ate it,' was his solemn response.
'Little Johnny, I've been a teacher for eighteen years. Do you really expect me to believe that?'
'It's true, Miss Martin, I swear,' insisted Little Johnny. 'I had to force him, but he ate it!'

Little Johnny was having a blazing row with his parents and cried, 'I want excitement, adventure, money and beautiful women. I'll never find it here at home, so I'm leaving. Don't try and stop me!' With that he headed toward the door.
His father rose and followed close behind.
'Didn't you hear what I said? I don't want you to try and stop me.'
'Who's trying to stop you?' replied his father. 'If you wait a minute, I'll go with you.'

Little Johnny turns up in his classroom one morning to be confronted by his teacher:

Teacher: 'Morning Johnny, and why
weren't you at school yesterday?'
Little Johnny: 'Well Miss, my Grandad got burnt.'
Teacher: 'Oh dear, he wasn't too badly hurt I hope?'
Little Johnny: 'Oh yes, Miss. They don't mess around
at those crematoriums.'

Little Johnny and his dad went to the supermarket and were in line at the checkout counter when Johnny says to his dad, 'Look at that lady in front of us, Daddy, she's fat.' The man notices the lady but politely tells Little Johnny, 'That's not a nice thing to say'. Little Johnny continued to stare and point and then said, 'No Daddy, she's really fat.' The man said, 'Please son, we're almost done here, behave and stop saying those things'. Just then the lady's mobile phone went off and Little Johnny said, 'Watch out dad, she's backing up!'

'I really worry that I shall never meet
you in Heaven Little Johnny,'
the teacher said.
'Oh, how come?' Johnny replied,
'What sin have you committed?'

Little Johnny was welcoming a new boy into his playgroup. 'How old are you?' Little Johnny asked.
'I don't know,' the new kid replied shrugging his shoulders.
'Well, do women bother you?' Little Johnny wanted to know. 'No,' the kid said confidently.
'Then you're five.'

Little Johnny and his four-year-old brother Joel were sitting together in church. Joel giggled, sang, and talked out loud. Finally, his big brother had had enough. 'You're not supposed to talk out loud in church,' warned Little Johnny. 'Why? Who's going to stop me?' Joel asked. Johnny pointed to the back of the church and said, 'See those two men standing by the door? They're hushers.'

When Little Johnny opened a birthday gift from his grandmother, he discovered a water pistol. He squealed with delight and headed for the sink. His mother was not so pleased. She turned to the grandmother and said, 'I'm surprised at you. Don't you remember how we used to drive you crazy with water guns?' Her mother smiled and then replied, 'I remember'.

A young mother paying a visit to a doctor friend and his wife made no attempt to restrain Little Johnny, who was ransacking an adjoining room. But finally, an extra loud clatter of bottles did prompt her to say, 'I hope, doctor, you don't mind Little Johnny being in there.' 'No,' said the doctor calmly, 'He'll be quiet when he gets to the poisons.'

Five-year-old Little Johnny said grace at family dinner one night. 'Dear God, thank you for this roast beef.' When he concluded, his parents asked him why he thanked God for roast beef when they were having chicken. Little Johnny smiled and said, 'I thought I'd see if He was paying attention tonight.'

Little Johnny had been misbehaving and was sent to his room. After a while he emerged and informed his mother that he had thought it over and then said a prayer.

'Fine', said the pleased mother. 'If you ask God to help you not misbehave, He will help you.'
'Oh, I didn't ask Him to help me not misbehave,' said Little Johnny. 'I asked Him to help you put up with me.'

'Dad,' said Little Johnny, 'I'm late for football practice. Would you please do my homework for me?' Little Johnny's father said irately, 'Son, it just wouldn't be right.' 'That's okay,' replied Little Johnny 'At least you could try?'

It was Little Johnny's first visit to the country, and feeding the chickens fascinated him. Early one morning he caught his first glimpse of a peacock strutting in the yard. Rushing indoors excitedly, Little Johnny sought his grandmother. 'Oh, Granny,' he exclaimed, 'One of the chickens is in bloom!'

**Little Johnny and his little sister are reading the book _Life of Animals_. Suddenly they jump from the sofa and run to their grandmother.
'Grandma, Grandma, can you have children?'
'Oh my dear, of course not, certainly not.'
Little Johnny turns to his little sister and says triumphantly 'I told you she is a male!'**

Finding one of her pupils making faces at others on the playground, Ms Smith stopped to gently reprove the child. Smiling sweetly the teacher said, 'When I was a child, I was told if I made ugly faces I would stay like that.'
Little Johnny looked up and replied, 'Well you can't say you weren't warned.'

'So your mother says your prayers for you each night. That's very commendable. What does she say?' The vicar asked the

little boy.
'Thank God he's in bed!'

Little Johnny asked his Sunday school teacher, 'Do you think
Noah did a lot of fishing when he was on the Ark?'
The teacher said, 'I imagine he did'.
Little Johnny replied, 'Well, he couldn't have caught many,
with only two worms.'

**'Mum, teacher was asking me today if I have any brothers or
sister who will be coming to school,'
said the boy to his mother,
'That's nice of her to take such an interest, dear. What did
she say when you told her you are the only child?'
'Thank goodness!'**

'Teacher, could anyone be punished for something that he'd
never done?' asked the boy
'Of course not! But why do you ask like that?'
'I didn't do my homework, sir!'

**'What are you doing under your desk?'
demanded the teacher.
'Didn't you tell us to read Jekyll and hide?'**

My granddaughter came to spend a few weeks with me, and I
decided to teach her to sew. After I had gone through a
lengthy explanation of how to thread the machine, she stepped
back, put her hands on her hips, and said in disbelief,
'You mean you can do all that, but you can't operate my
Game Boy?'

**My grandmother moved in with our family of five.
As I was brushing my teeth one morning, she tapped on the
door. 'Is anyone in there?' she called.**

I mumbled an answer, to which she replied,
'Is that a yes or a no?'

Two little boys were visiting their grandfather and he took
them to a restaurant for lunch. They couldn't make up their
minds about what they wanted to eat.
Finally the grandfather grinned at the server and said,
'Just bring them bread and water'.
One of the little boys looked up and quavered, 'Can I have
ketchup on it?'

**The advice your son rejected is now being given by him to
your grandson.**

Working mothers are guinea pigs in a scientific experiment to
show that sleep is not necessary to human life.

**Parents often talk about the younger generations as if they
didn't have anything to do with it.**

Fathers of 1906 didn't have it nearly as good as fathers of
today; but they did have a few advantages:

**In 1906, fathers prayed their children would learn English.
Today, fathers pray their children will speak English.**

In 1906, a father waited for the doctor to tell him when the
baby arrived. Today, a father must wear a smock, know how to
breathe, and make sure film is in the video camera.

**In 1906, fathers passed on clothing to their sons.
Today, kids wouldn't touch Dad's clothes if they were
sliding naked down a glacier.**

In 1906, fathers could count on children to join the family business. Today, fathers pray their kids will soon come home from university long enough to teach them how to work the computer and set the DVD.

In 1906, a father smoked a pipe.
If he tries that today, he gets sent outside after a lecture on lip cancer.

In 1906, a father came home from work to find his wife and children at the supper table.
Today, a father comes home to a note: 'Jimmy's at football, Cindy's at gymnastics, I'm out with the girls, pizza in fridge.'

In 1906, fathers and sons would have heart-to-heart conversations while fishing in a stream.
Today, fathers pluck the headphones off their sons' ears and shout, 'WHEN YOU HAVE A MINUTE...'

In 1906, if a father had breakfast in bed, it was eggs and bacon and ham and potatoes.
Today, it's muesli, soya milk, dry toast and a lecture on cholesterol.

In 1906, a happy meal was when Father shared funny stories around the table.
Today, a happy meal is what Dad buys at McDonald's.

In 1906, when fathers entered the room,
children often rose to attention.
Today, kids glance up and grunt, 'Dad, you're
invading my space'.

**In 1906, fathers threatened their daughter's suitors with
shotguns if the girl came home late.
Today, fathers break the ice by saying, 'So ... how long have
you had those body piercings?'**

SOME THINGS OUR MOTHER WOULD NEVER SAY
'How on earth can you see the TV sitting so far back?'
**'Just leave all the lights on, it makes the house look more
cheery.'**
'Let me smell that t-shirt. Yes, it's okay for another week.'

**MORE THINGS YOUR MOTHER WOULD NEVER SAY
'Go ahead and keep that stray dog, darling. I'll be glad
to feed and walk him every day.'**
'I don't have a tissue with me, just use your sleeve.'
**'Don't bother wearing a jacket, the wind-chill is
bound to improve.'**

A man passed out in a dead faint as he came out of his front
door onto the porch. When the paramedics arrived, they
helped him regain consciousness and asked if he knew what
caused him to faint. 'It was enough to make anybody faint,' he
said. 'My son asked me for the keys to the garage, and instead
of driving the car out, he came out with the lawn mower.'

**When our second child was on the way, my wife and I
attended a pre-birth class aimed at couples who had already
had at least one child. The instructor raised the issue of
breaking the news to the older child. It went like this:**

'Some parents,' she said, 'tell the older child, "We love you so much we decided to bring another child into this family." But think about that. Ladies, what if your husband came home one day and said, "Honey, I love you so much I decided to bring home another wife." One of the women spoke up immediately. 'Does she cook?'

An educational psychologist was sat in a café preparing his notes for a lecture he was going to give to parents. An elderly woman sitting next to him explained that she was returning home after having spent two weeks visiting her six children, 18 grandchildren and 10 great-grandchildren. Then she enquired what the man did for a living. He told her, fully expecting her to question him for free professional advice. Instead she sat back, picked up a magazine and said, 'If there's anything you want to know, just ask me.'

There is always a lot to be thankful for if you take the time to look. I'm sitting here thinking how nice it is that wrinkles don't hurt.

According to the pre-natal classes, it's not pain that I'll feel during labour, but pressure. Is she right? Yes, in the same way that a tornado might be called an air current.

'Daddy,' a little girl asked her father, 'do all fairy tales begin with "Once upon a time"?' 'No, sweetheart,' he answered. 'Some begin with 'If I am elected.'"

The best way to keep kids at home is to make a pleasant atmosphere and let the air out of their tyres.

A woman meant to call a record shop but dialled
the wrong number and got a private number instead.
'Do you have "Eyes of Blue" and "A Love Supreme"?" she asked.
'Well, no,' answered the puzzled homeowner. 'But I have a
wife and eleven children.'

'Is that a record?' she
enquired.
'I don't think so,'
replied the man,
'but it's as close as I
want to get.'

Middle age is when
you choose your
cereal for the fibre,
not the toy.

Families are like
fudge, mostly sweet,
with a few nuts.

Little Johnny was in church with his mother for Sunday service
when he felt a sudden urge to be sick.
'Mum, I think I'm going to throw up!'
She told him, 'I want you to run outside as fast as you can.
Run across the lawn and go behind the bushes. You can throw
up behind the bushes and nobody will see you.'
So Little Johnny ran for the door. Less than a minute later,
he returned to his seat next to his mum. He had the look of
obvious relief on his young face.
'Did you make it all the way to the bushes, Johnny?'
'I didn't have to go that far, mum. Just as I got to the front
door, I found a box that had a sign on it: FOR THE SICK.'

'Mummy, mummy, does a lemon have a beak?'
'No it doesn't.'
'Oops, so it was a canary that I squeezed.'

Computer games don't affect kids. If Pacman had affected us
as children, we would now run around in darkened rooms,
munching pills and listening to repetitive music.

Little Susie was watching her father, a vicar, write a sermon.
'How do you know what to say?' she asked.
'Why, God tells me.'
'Oh, then why do you keep crossing things out?'

The whole class was on a trip to the fire station.
The firefighter giving the presentation held up a smoke
detector and asked the class, 'Does anyone know what this is?'
A little boy's hand shot up and the fire fighter called on him.
'That's how Mummy knows supper is ready!'

A child comes home from his first day at school.
Mother asks, 'What did you learn today?'
'Not enough. I have to go back tomorrow.'

A woman of 35 thinks of having children.
What does a man of 35 think of? Dating younger women.

A Sunday school teacher asked, 'And why is it necessary to
be quiet in church?'
A little boy replied, 'Because people are sleeping.'

Single women claim that all the good men are married, while
all married women complain about their lousy husbands.
This confirms that there is no such thing as a good man.

'What kind of person is your new boyfriend? Is he respectable?' Asked the father.
'Of course he is, Dad He's thrifty, doesn't drink or smoke, has a very nice wife and three well-behaved children.'

What's the quickest way to lose 190 pounds of ugly fat?
Divorce him.

**What's the difference between a man and a messy room?
You can straighten up a messy room.**

A man had his credit card stolen. He however decided not to report it because the thief was spending less than his wife did.

**Why does it take one million sperm to fertilize one egg?
They won't stop to ask directions.**

Men are like computers: hard to figure out and never have enough memory.

**How are men like noodles?
They are always in hot water, they lack taste,
and they need dough.**

What's the difference between a man and a parrot?
You can teach a parrot to talk nicely.

**What do you do if your best friend runs off with your husband?
Miss her. Pity her.**

Did you hear about the woman who finally figured out men?
She died laughing before she could tell anybody.

**If a man is alone in the forest, and he says something, and
there's no woman there to disagree with him.
Is he still wrong?**

What's the difference between an intelligent man and a UFO?
I don't know, I've never seen either one.

**We try to keep him out of the kitchen.
Last time he cooked he burned the salad.**

Why don't men cook at home?
No one's invented a steak that will fit in the toaster.

**Why is a man different from a computer?
You only have to tell the computer once.**

**Why do men like love at first sight?
It saves them a lot of time.**

What is the most common pregnancy craving?
For men to be the ones who get pregnant.

**Why don't men often show their true feelings?
Because they don't have any.**

Why is a man like the weather?
Nothing can be done to change either one of them.

**What is the only time a man thinks
about a candlelight dinner?
When the power goes off.**

My husband said he wanted more space.
So I locked him outside.

Two musicians are walking down the street, and one says to the other, 'Who was that piccolo I saw you with last night?' The other replies, 'That was no piccolo, that was my fife.'

If at first you don't succeed, shouldn't you try doing it like your wife told you to do it?

A man gets home, screeches his car into the driveway, runs into the house, slams the door and shouts to his wife at the top of his lungs, 'Pack your bags. I won the lottery!'
The wife says, 'Oh my God! What should I pack, beach stuff or mountain stuff?'
'Doesn't matter,' he says. 'Just get the hell out.'

An elderly lady called the police on her mobile phone to report that her car has been broken into.
She is hysterical as she explains her situation to the call centre:
'They've stolen the stereo, the steering wheel, the brake pedal and even the accelerator!'
'Stay calm. An officer is on the way.'
Within minutes, the officer radios in.
'Disregard the call,' he says. 'She got in the back seat by mistake.'

My wife and I have the secret to making a marriage last.
Twice a week, we go to a nice restaurant and have a little wine and good food.
She goes on Tuesdays and I go on Fridays.

'Darling,' whispered a frail little husband from his chair.
'I'm very sick, would you please call me a vet?'
'A vet? Why do you want a vet and not a medical doctor?' asked his wife.
The husband replied, 'Because I work like a horse, live like a dog, and have to sleep with a silly cow!'

During their first date, a man goes to a girl's house, and she shows him into the living room. She excuses herself to go to get them a drink, and as he's standing there alone, he notices a little vase on the mantel. He picks it up, and as he's looking at it, she walks back in with the drinks.
Holding up the vase, he asks, 'What's this?'
She says, 'Oh, my father's ashes are in there.'
He goes, 'I ... I didn't know your father.'
'Yes, he's too lazy to go to the kitchen to get an ashtray.'

Two mothers met for coffee one morning, and the conversation naturally turned to their kids.
'Well, Susan, how are your kids?' asks Linda.
'To tell you the truth', says Susan, 'my John has married a witch! She doesn't get out of bed until eleven. She's out all day spending his money on Heaven knows what, and when he gets home, exhausted, does she have a nice hot dinner for him? NO! She makes him take her out to dinner at an expensive restaurant.'
'Hmmm ... and how is your daughter?' Linda asks.
'Ah!' says Susan. 'Lisa has married a saint! He brings her breakfast in bed, he gives her enough money to buy all she needs, and in the evening he takes her out to dinner at a nice, fancy restaurant.'

A boy was taking care of his baby sister while his parents went to town shopping. He decided to go fishing and he had to take her along.
'I'll never take her along with me again!' he told his mother that evening. 'I didn't catch a thing!'
'Oh, next time I'm sure she'll be quiet and not scare the fish away,' his mother said.
The boy said, 'It wasn't that. She ate all the bait.'

LIGHT-BULB JOKES

How many actors does it take to change a light bulb?
Only one, they don't like to share the spotlight.

**How many civil servants does it take
to screw in a light bulb?
Two, one to screw it in and one to screw it up.**

How many conservatives does it take to change a light bulb?
Four, one to change it and three to complain that the old light
bulb was a lot better than the new one.

**How many moaning grand parents does it take
to change a light bulb?
Don't worry about us, we'll sit in the dark.**

How many teenagers does it take to screw in a light bulb?
One, but they'll be on the phone for five hours telling their
friends about it.

**How many Blue Peter presenters does it take
to change a light bulb?
Two, one to change the light bulb and the other to say
'here's one we did earlier'.**

How many civil servants does it take to change a light bulb?
Forty-five, one to change the light bulb
and 44 to process the paperwork.

**How many dull people does it take
to change a light bulb?
One.**

How many Mafia hit men does it take to change a light bulb?
Three, one to screw it in, one to watch
and one to shoot the witness.

How many waiters does it take
to change a light bulb?
None, even a broken light bulb
can't catch their eye.

How many babysitters does it take
to change a light bulb?
None, they don't make nappies
that small.

How many SAS men does it take
to change a light bulb?
Two, one to change it
one to shout 'Go, Go, Go!'

How many psychiatrists does it take to change a light bulb?
Only one, but the bulb has got to really want to change.

How many pessimists does it take to change a light bulb?
None, because the new bulb probably won't work either.

How many optimists does it take to change a light bulb?
None, because they are convinced the electricity
will come back on again soon.

How many circus performers does it take
to change a light bulb?
Four, one to change the bulb and three to sing, 'Ta da!'

How many Green Peace supporters does it take
to change a light bulb?
Two, one to put in the new one
and another to recycle the old one.

How many monkeys does it take to change a light bulb?
Two, one to do it and one to scratch his bum.

How many lawyers does it take to change a light bulb?
How many can you afford?

How many sheep does it take to change a light bulb?
Twenty-one, one to change it and 20 to follow him
around while he looks for a new one.

How many Californians does it take to change a light bulb?
Six, one to turn the bulb, one for support and four to relate to
the experience.

How many psychiatrists does it take to change a light bulb?
None, the bulb will change itself when it's ready.

How many stupid people does it take to screw in a light bulb?
Ten, one to hold the bulb and nine to rotate the ladder.

How many nuclear engineers does it take
to change a light bulb?
Seven, one to install the new bulb, and six to work out
what to do with the old one for the next 10,000 years.

How many male chauvinistic pigs does it take
to change a light bulb?
None let her cook in the dark.

How many 'Real Men' does it take to change a light bulb?
None, 'Real Men' aren't afraid of the dark.

How many 'Real Women' does it take to change a light bulb?
None, a 'Real Woman' would have plenty of
'Real Men' around to do it for them.

How many computer-
hardware specialists
does it take to change
a light bulb?
None. That's a software
problem.

How many computer-
hardware sales people
does it take to change
a light bulb?
None, they just have
marketing portray the dead
bulb as a feature.

How many software designers does it take
to screw in a light bulb?
None. That's a hardware problem.

How many Virgin airline employees does it take to
change a light bulb?
Four, one to screw it in and three to design the tee shirts.

How many Feminists does it take to change a light bulb?
That's not funny!

How many Surrealists does it take to change a light bulb?
Two, one to hold the giraffe, and the other to fill the shower
with brightly coloured globes.

How many doctors does it take to screw in a light bulb?
Three, one to find a bulb specialist, one to find a bulb
installation specialist, and one to write out the bill.

How many policemen does it take to change a light bulb?
None, it turned itself in.

How many board meetings does it take
to get a light bulb changed?
This topic was resumed from last week's discussion,
but is incomplete pending resolution of some action items.

How many accountants does it take to change a light bulb?
What kind of answer did you have in mind?

How many accountants does it take to change a light bulb?
I'm afraid that's not a budgeted item.

How many junkies does it take to change a light bulb?
'Oh wow, is it like dark, man?'

How many pygmies does it take to change a light bulb?
At least three.

How many mystery writers does it take
to change a light bulb?
Two, one to screw it almost all the way in
and the other to give it a surprising twist at the end.

How many bikers does it take to change a light bulb?
Two, one to change the bulb, and the other to kick the switch.

How many business consultants does it take
to change a light bulb?
We don't know, they never get past the feasibility study.

How many stockbrokers does it take to change a light bulb?
Two, one to take out the bulb and drop it,
and the other to try and sell it before it crashes.

How many aides to the US President does it take
to change a light bulb?
None, they like to keep him in the dark.

How many vampires does it take to change a light bulb?
None, they like it in the dark.

How many DIY enthusiasts does it take to
change a light bulb?
Only one, but it takes him two weekends and three trips to
the DIY superstore.

How many policemen does it take to screw in a light bulb?
Just one, but he is never around when you need him.

How many doctors does it take to screw in a light bulb?
Only one, but he has to have a nurse to tell him
which end to screw in.

How many surgeons does it take to change a light bulb?
None, they would wait for a suitable donor
and do a filament transplant.

How many chiropractors does it take to change a light bulb?
Only one, but it takes nine visits.

How many Bill Gates does it take to change a light bulb?
None, he simply declares darkness to be the new standard.

How many social scientists does it take
to change a light bulb?
They do not change light bulbs; they search for the root
cause as to why the last one went out.

How many economists does it take to change a light bulb?
That depends on the wage rate.

**How many members of the USS Enterprise
does it take to change a light bulb?
All of them. Bones to say 'Its dead Jim', Uhura to send a
distress signal, Sulu to listen to Chekov saying 'Light bulbs
vere really an old Russian invention', Spock to be fascinated
by the illogical early demise of the light bulb, Scotty to do
the work, and Kirk to get the girl.**

How many publishers does it take to screw in a light bulb?
Two, one to change the bulb and one to issue a rejection slip
to the old bulb.

**How many economists does it take to screw in a light bulb?
None, if the light bulb really needed changing,
market forces would have already caused it to happen.**

How many mutants does it take to change a light bulb?
Two-thirds.

**How many waitresses does it take to change a light bulb?
Three, two to stand around complaining about it
and one to go get the manager.**

How many lumberjacks does it take to change a light bulb?
One, but he uses a chainsaw.

**How many cafeteria staff does it take to change a light bulb?
Sorry, we closed 18 seconds ago, and I've just cashed up.**

How many art directors does it take to change a light bulb?
Does it have to be a light bulb?

How many pawnbrokers does it take to change a light bulb?
None, it's of no interest to them.

How many London taxi drivers does it take
to change a light bulb?
What? Go all the way up there and come back empty?
You must be jokin' mate!

How many archaeologists does it take
to change a light bulb?
Three, one to change it and two to argue about
how old the old one is.

How many historic-building preservation officers
does it take to change a light bulb?
One, but it takes a year to find an antique light bulb
so it'll be architecturally accurate.

How many aerobics instructors does it take
to change a light bulb?
Five, four to do it in perfect synchrony and one to stand
there going 'To the left, and to the left, and to the left, and
to the left, and take it out, and put it down, and pick it up,
and put it in...'

How many Einsteins does it take to change a light bulb?
That depends on the speed of the changer and the
mass of the bulb.

How many schizophrenics does it take
to change a light bulb?
Well, he thinks it's five but as we all now it's only him,
so it's only one really.

How many rottweilers does it take to change a light bulb? Make me!

How many dachsunds does it take to change a light bulb? You know I can't possibly get up there.

How many greyhounds does it take to change a light bulb? Who cares? It's not a rabbit.

How many marketing directors does it take to change a light bulb? It isn't too late to make this neon instead, is it?

How many proofreaders does it take to change a light bulb? Proofreaders aren't supposed to change light bulbs. They should just query them.

How many publishers does it take to screw in a light bulb? Three, one to screw it in and two to hold down the author.

How many social workers does it take to change a light bulb? Four. One to remove the bulb from the socket and take it away without checking whether or not there was actually anything wrong with it, one to accuse its owners of mistreating it, one to find somewhere else to screw it in for the next six months, and one to eventually bring it back and say it was all done with the light bulb's best interests at heart.

How many social workers does it take to change a light bulb?

Four, one to change the bulb, one to counsel the old bulb
because it's been thrown away by an uncaring society,
one to arrange the case conference and one to make sure
they are all following the correct working practice.

How many running-dog lackeys of the bourgeoisie does it take
to change a light bulb?
Two, one to exploit the proletariat and one
to control the means of production.

How many bureaucrats does it take to screw in a light bulb?
Five, one to change the light bulb and the other four to fill
out the Environmental Impact Statement.

How many IKEA shop assistants does it take
to change a light bulb?
'Sorry, we ran out of light bulb stock.
We expect it to arrive early next month.'

How many copyeditors does it take to screw in a light bulb?
The last time this question was asked, it involved art
directors. Is the difference intentional? Should one or the
other instance be changed? It seems inconsistent.

How many President Kennedy assassination conspiracy
theorists does it take to screw in a light bulb?
Fifteen. One to screw it in, five to say he acted alone,
one to say that someone hidden in the ceiling helped,
one to film it, one to do an intense examination of the
film and conclude the first screwer did not act alone,
one to insist that the bulb was altered after it was unscrewed,
three tramps to walk across the room an hour later,
one to insist LBJ really screwed the bulb in, and one
to accuse all the others of being disinformation specialists.

How many bankers does it take to change a light bulb?
None, bankers don't change light bulbs.

How many bankers does it take to change a light bulb?
Four, one to hold the bulb and three to try to
remember the combination.

How many mean people does it take to change a light bulb?
Two, one to change it, and one to complain that a light bulb
still only lasts 1,000 hours.

How many European ballet dancers does it take
to screw in a light bulb?
None, they like Danzig in the dark.

How many Seventies disco dancers does it take
to change a light bulb?
Two, one to boogie up the ladder
and one to say 'Get daaowwwwn!'

How many Chinese people does it take to change a light bulb?
Thousands, because Confucius say
many hands make light work.

How many pizza-delivery men does it take
to change a light bulb?
Two, one to change it and one to sprinkle it
with Parmesan.

How many protestors does it take to screw in a light bulb?
Two, one to screw it in, and a second to hand out leaflets

How many health and safety inspectors does it take to
change a light bulb?
Four, one to change it and three to hold the ladder.

How many special-service agents does it take to
screw in a light bulb?
Six, four to storm the room and take control of it, one to
forcibly eject the old bulb, and another one to screw it in.

**How many Australians does it take to screw in a light bulb?
Two, one to say 'She'll be right mate'
and one to fetch the beers.**

How many armies does it take to change a light bulb?
At least five. The Germans to start it, the French
to give up really easily after only trying for a
little while, the Italians to make a start, get nowhere,
and then try again from the other side,
the Americans to turn up late and finish it off
and take all the credit, and the Swiss to pretend
nothing out of the ordinary is happening.

**How many unemployed people does it take
to screw in a light bulb?
One, but 200 had to apply for the job.**

How many terrorists does it take to change a light bulb?
One hundred. One to screw it in and 99
to hold the house hostage.

**How many terrorists does it take to change a light bulb?
Six, one to change the bulb, and five to take the credit
when it explodes.**

How many terrorists does it take to change a light bulb?
Two, one to stage a suicide attack on the bulb and another to
claim responsibility in a phone call to the media.

How many McDonald's employees does it take
to change a light bulb?
Two, one to change it and one
to ask whether you'd like fries with it.

One.
How many psychics does it take to change a light bulb?

**How many members of the
royal family does it take
to screw in a light bulb?
'Actually none. As your queen
I would like to reassure the
people of the commonwealth
that while our family may have
had our Annus Horribilis, none
of us, to my knowledge, have
actually screwed in a light bulb.'**

How many Victorians does it
take to screw in a light bulb?
We do not discuss this with ladies
and children present.

**How many Gestapo
interrogators does it take to
screw in a light bulb?
Ve are asking ze qvestions!**

How many programmers does it
take to change a light bulb?
Five, two to write the specification program, one to screw it in,
and two to explain why the project was late.

How many programmers does it take to change a light bulb?
It's hard to say. Each time we separate the bulb into its
modules to do unit testing, it stops working.

How many programmers does it take to change a light bulb?
None. It's not a bug, it's a feature.

How many programmers does it take to change a light bulb?
Four, one to design the change, one to implement it, one to
document it, and one to maintain it afterwards.

How many Yorkshiremen does it take to change a light bulb?
Four, one to change it, one to hold his racing pigeon, one to
hold his greyhound, and one to drink his pint of bitter.

How many PC users does it take to change a light bulb?
Two, one to do it, and one to check the new bulb for viruse.

How many strike-factory employees does it take
to change a light bulb?
None, the replacement bulbs have refused to cross
the union picket lines.

How many carpenters does it take to screw in a light bulb?
That's the electrician's job.

How many first-time computer users does it take
to screw in a light bulb?
One, but it takes him three hours and two phone calls to the
electrician before he realizes he forgot to turn the switch on.

How many software engineers does it take
to change a light bulb?
None: 'We'll document it in the user manual.'

How many trainspotters does it take to change a light bulb?
Three, one to change it, one to write its number down, and
one to bring the anoraks and the flask of soup.

**How many tourists does it take to change a light bulb?
Six, one to hold the bulb and five to ask for directions.**

How many Norwegians does is take to change a light bulb?
Two, one to screw in the bulb and one to tell
a long story about it.

**How many public-opinion researchers does it take
to screw in a light bulb?
With what degree of certainty do you need to know?**

How many battery chickens does it take
to change a light bulb?
Twenty-one, one to change the bulb,
and 20 to provide the current.

**How many elephants does it take to change a light bulb?
Two, but it has to be a pretty big light bulb.**

How many gas fitters does it take to change a light bulb?
Three, one to turn up the day before when you're out, one to
change the switch, and one to bring along
the wrong kind of bulb.

**How many dogs does it take to change a light bulb?
Two, one to change it, and one to sniff the other's bum.**

How many cats does it take to change a light bulb?
Just one. As long as she can get under your feet and trip you
up while you're changing it.

How many antelopes does it take to change a light bulb?
None, they are hardy animals that migrate between tundra
and wide-open plains and therefore have no need for an
artificial light source.

How many drummers does it take to change a light bulb?
Only one, but he'll break 10 bulbs before figuring out that they
can't just be pushed in.

**How many drummers does it take to change a light bulb?
None, they have a machine that does that now.**

How many folk musicians it takes to change a light bulb?
They don't. They only use acoustic light bulbs.

**How many Pop Idol contestants does it take
to change a light bulb?
They can't sing, they can't dance, so what makes you think
they can change a light bulb?**

How many bass guitarists does it take to screw in a light bulb?
Five, one to do it and four to beat back all the guitarists who
are trying to elbow him out of the spotlight.

**How many female opera singers does it take
to change a light bulb?
None. If they sing loudly enough they'll break it.**

How many university students does it take
to change a light bulb?
Only one, but it may take upwards of five years
for him to get it done.

How many university students does it take
to screw in a light bulb?
It all depends on the size of the grant.

Do you know how many musicians it takes
to change a light bulb?
Five, one to change the bulb and four to get in free because
they know the guy who owns the socket.

How many student accommodation landlords does it take
to screw in a light bulb?
None. The students will just wreck it anyhow, so why bother?

How many university students does it take
to change a light bulb?
Two, one to fuse all the electrics while doing something silly,
and one to phone the landlord to ask for
the light bulb to be changed.

How many roadies does it take to change a light bulb?
None. 'I don't do lights. That's the light crew's job.'

How many Americans does it take to change a light bulb ?
250,000,000, one to change it and 249,999,999 to debate
whether it was politically correct.

How many witches does it take to change a light bulb?
It depends on what you want them to change it into.

How many egotists does it take to change a light bulb?
One. He holds on to the light bulb, and waits for the world to
revolve around him.

How many roadies does it take to change a light bulb?
One, two! One, two! One, two!

How many Goths does it take to change a light bulb?
None. They prefer everything all black anyway.

**How many academics does it take to change a light bulb?
None, that's what research students are for.**

How many academics does it take to change a light bulb?
Five, one to write the grant proposal, one to do the
mathematical modelling, one to type the research paper,
one to submit the paper for publishing, and one
to hire a student to do the work.

**How many schoolteachers does it take to
change a light bulb?
One if at home, but if in work time, four.**

How many vets does it take to change a
light bulb?
Three, one to change the bulb and two
more to complain that a doctor makes 10
times as much for the same procedure.

**How many dentists does it take to
change a light bulb ?
Three, one to administer the
anaesthetic, one to extract the light
bulb, and one to offer the socket some vile
pink mouthwash.**

How many doctors does it take
to screw in a light bulb?
None, they only sign the
death certificate.

**How many doctors does it take to screw in a light bulb?
Nurse!**

How many jugglers does it take to change a light bulb?
One, but they like to show off and use four light bulbs.

**How many trades unionists does it take
to change a light bulb?
None. They cannot interfere with the light bulb's
inalienable right to withdraw its labour.**

How many politically correct people does it take
to change a light bulb?
None. 'Why should we impose our values on the light bulb?
If it wishes to be a light bulb of no light, we should respect its
uniqueness and individuality.'

**How many residents of country towns does it take
to screw in a light bulb?
None, they're afraid there's been
too much development already.**

How many philosophers does it take to change a light bulb?
That's an interesting question isn't it?

**How many philosophers does it take to change a light bulb?
Three, one to change it and two to stand around arguing
over whether or not the light bulb exists.**

How many philosophers does it take to change a light bulb?
Define 'light bulb'.

**How many lexicographers does it take
to change a light bulb?**

Two, one to change it and one to protest that he should
have changed it to 'lightbulb'.

How many fatalists does it take to screw in a light bulb?
We're all going to die anyway!

How many physiotherapists does it take
to change a light bulb?
None, they just give the dead bulb some exercises to do and
hope it will be working a bit better the next time they see it.

How many accident and emergency doctors does it take
to change a light bulb ?
One, but the bulb will have to wait three hours to be changed.

How many NHS hospital staff does it take
to change a light bulb?
Six, one to diagnose the problem, one to take an X-ray,
one to wheel in the replacement on a trolley, one to apply
an anaesthetic, one to do the delicate operation,
and one to examine the late bulb in a post-mortem.

How many Daleks does it take to change a light bulb?
A million to conquer a race that can climb ladders for them.

How many Daleks does it take to change a light bulb?
Daleks don't change light bulbs – they level the building.

How many junkies does it take to screw in a light bulb?
Two, one to roll it, and one to light it up.

How many WWF wrestlers does it take
to change a light bulb?
Five, one to change it four to fake it.

How many football players does it take to screw in a light bulb?
Five, one to get into position to screw it in,
one to kick the legs out from under him, one to snatch the
light bulb and pass it to his mate who, then goes
and screws it in over the other side of the room,
and one to roll around on the floor pretending to be injured.

**How many soccer players does it take to
screw in a light bulb?
Fifteen, one to put the bulb in, 10 to kiss him afterwards,
and the other side's back four to all stand around and put
their hands up claiming it was offside.**

How many talk-show hosts does it take to change a light bulb?
Three, one to screw in the new bulb, one to
ask the old one how it feels to be replaced,
and one to take questions from the audience.

**How many chickens does it take to screw in a light bulb?
Two, one to do it and one to cross the road.**

How many chickens does it take to screw in a light bulb?
Just one, and she will only screw it in as soon as she decides it
isn't going to hatch.

**How many chickens does it take to screw in a light bulb?
None, they're all far too busy crossing the road.**

How many librarians does it take to screw in a light bulb?
I don't know, but I can look it up for you.

**How many KGB agents does it take to change a light bulb?
Two, one to screw it in and the other
to check it for microphones.**

How many light bulbs does it take to change a light bulb?
Two, the new one and the old one.

**How many scrabble players does it take
to change a lightbulb?
I don't actually know, but it's on a triple word score anyway.**

How many dyslexics does it take to bulb a light change?
Ten, one to change the light bulb and
nine to misread the manual.

**How many dyslexics does it take to bulb a light change?
Eno.**

How many politicians does it take to change a light bulb?
Two, one to change it, and another one to change it back again.

**How many politicians does it take to change a light bulb?
Four, one to change it and the other three to deny it.**

How many MPs does it take to change a light bulb?
Twenty-one, one to change it and 20 to form a fact-finding
committee to learn more about how it's done.

**How many MPs does it take to change a light bulb?
I can't tell you that, the light-bulb changing service
has been privatized and the information you require is
commercially sensitive.**

How many city people does it take to screw in a light bulb?
Four, one to do it and three not to get involved.

**How many rich people does it take to change a light bulb?
Two, one to do it and the other to steady the chandelier.**

How many paranoid people does it take to change a light bulb?
Why, who wants to know?

**How many paranoid people does it take to change a light bulb?
Just what exactly do you mean by that?**

How many quality-assurance managers does it take
to change a light bulb?
We have formed a quality circle to study the problem of why light
bulbs burn out and to determine the best thing we as managers
can do to enable light bulbs to work smarter, not harder.

**How many admin assistants does it take
to change a light bulb?
None. I can't do anything unless you complete a light bulb
design-change request form.**

How many gardeners does it
take to change a light bulb?
Three, one to change it
and two to have a debate
about whether this is the
right time of year to be
putting in light bulbs
or daffodil bulbs.

How many mail-order catalogue employees does it take to change a light bulb?
We can change the bulb in 7–10 working days; if you call before 2 p.m. and pay extra we can get the bulb changed overnight.

How many journalists does it take to screw in a light bulb?
Three, one to report it as an inspired government programme to bring light to the people, one to report it as a diabolical government plot to deprive the poor of darkness, and one to win a prestigious prize for reporting that the electric company hired a light-bulb assassin to break the bulb in the first place.

How many managers does it take to change a light bulb?
Three, one to get the bulb and two to get the phone number to dial one of their subordinates to actually change it.

How many Bob Dylan fans does it take to
screw in a light bulb?
The answer, my friend, is blowin' in the wind. The answer is blowin' in the wind.

How many punks does it take to change a light bulb?
Two, one to screw in the bulb and the other to smash the old one on his forehead.

How many medical students does it take
to change a light bulb?
None, they're too busy propping up the bar.

How many computer-studies students does it take
to change a light bulb?
None, they're far too busy hacking.

How many Hari Krishnas does it take to screw in a light bulb?
Ten, one to do it and the rest to dance around, play the
tambourine, chant and sing.

How many wives does it take to change a light bulb?
Nobody knows, they're too busy
trying to change their husbands.

MISCELLANEOUS JOKES

What do computer operators eat for lunch?
Chips.

THE THREE LAWS OF SECURE COMPUTING
Don't buy a computer.
If you do buy a computer, don't plug it in.
If you do plug it in, sell it and return to step 1.

A young man professed the desire to become the world's greatest writer. His careers officer asked him to define the word 'great', to which he replied, 'I want to write words that the whole world will read and people will react to it on an emotional level. Things that will make them scream, cry, howl in pain and in anger,' he replied.
Ten years later he was writing error messages for Microsoft.

A woman calls the helpdesk as she is having problems with her printer. The helpdesk operator asks her if her computer is running under Windows. The woman replies, 'No, my desk is next to the door.'

A man walks into a Silicon Valley pet shop looking for a monkey. The storeowner points towards three identical-looking monkeys in politically correct, animal-friendly natural mini-habitats. 'The one to the left costs $500,' says the storeowner. 'Why so much?' asks the customer. 'Because it can program in C,' answers the storeowner. The customer inquires about the next monkey and is told, 'That one costs $1500, because it knows Visual C++ and Object-Relational technology.' The startled man then asks about the third monkey. 'That one costs $3000,' answers the storeowner. '$3000!' exclaims the man. 'What can that one do?' To which the owner replies, 'To be honest, I've never seen it do a single thing, but it calls itself a Consultant.'

Two programmers and their program manager are walking together during their lunch break when they come upon an old brass lamp. They pick it up and dust it off. Poof – out pops a genie. 'Thank you for releasing me from my lamp-prison. I can grant you three wishes. Since there are three of you I will grant one wish to each of you,' the genie says.

The first programmer thinks for a moment and says, 'I'd like to be sailing a yacht, racing before the wind, with an all-girl crew.'

'It is done', said the Genie, and the first programmer disappears. The second programmer thinks for a moment and says, 'I'd like to be riding my motorbike with a gang of beautiful women through the countryside.'

'It is done', said the Genie, and poof, the second programmer disappears. The program manager looks thoughtfully at where the other two had been standing. 'I'd like those two back in the office after lunch.'

FIVE REASONS TO BELIEVE COMPUTERS ARE MALE
They have a lot of data, but are still clueless.
They are supposed to help you solve problems, but half the time they are the problem.
As soon as you commit to one you realize that, if you had waited a little longer, you could have obtained a better model.
In order to get their attention, you have to turn them on.
Big power surges knock them out for the rest of the night.

FOUR REASONS TO BELIEVE COMPUTERS ARE FEMALE
No one but their creator understands their internal logic.
The native language they use to communicate with other computers is incomprehensible to everyone else.
Even your smallest mistakes are stored in long-term memory for later retrieval.

As soon as you make a commitment to one, you find yourself spending half your salary on accessories for it.

A computer programmer had been missing from work for over a week when finally someone noticed and called the police. They went round to his apartment and broke the door down. They found him dead in the still-running shower with an empty bottle of shampoo next to his body. Apparently he'd been washing his hair. The instructions on the bottle said:
Wet hair
Apply shampoo
Wait 2 minutes
Rinse
Repeat

A computer-support man goes to a firing range. He shoots 10 bullets at the target 50 metres away. The supervisors check the target and see that there's not even a single hit, and they shout to him that he has missed. So he tells them to recheck, and gets the same answer. Then he shoots again and when they tell him he's missed again he shouts back, 'I don't know why, it's working perfectly here, the problem must be yours.'

Life before computers meant that a cursor was someone who swore a lot.

Life before computers meant that if you unzipped something, you'd probably be arrested.

There was an engineer, manager and programmer driving down a steep mountain road. The brakes failed and the car careened down the road out of control. Half way down the driver managed to stop the car by running it against the embankment narrowly avoiding going over a cliff. They all got out, shaken by their narrow escape from death, but otherwise unharmed. The manager said, 'To fix this problem we need to organise a committee, have meetings, and through a process of continuous improvement, develop a solution.'
The engineer said 'No that would take too long, and besides that method never worked before.
I have my trusty pen knife here and will take apart the brake system, isolate the problem and correct it.'
The programmer said, 'I think you're both wrong!
I think we should all push the car back up the hill and see if it happens again.'

You know technology is taking over when you haven't played patience with a real pack of cards.

You know technology is taking over when you try to enter your password on the microwave.

An artist, a lawyer, and a computer scientist are discussing the merits of a mistress. The artist tells of the passion, the thrill that comes with the risk of being discovered. The lawyer warns of the difficulties. It can lead to guilt, divorce, and bankruptcy. Not worth it, too many problems. The computer scientist says, 'It's the best thing that's ever happened to me. My wife thinks I'm with my mistress. My mistress thinks I'm home with my wife, and I can spend all night on the computer!'

How does the barber cut the moon's hair?
Eclipse it.

What did one cloud say to the other?
Let's be cirrus.

Dad says to his little boy, 'See that man over there? He's six
feet in his socks.'
'Don't be daft dad, you'll be telling me next
he's two heads in his hat.'

'You don't look very happy son, what's wrong?'
'Well, mum said I could eat as many cakes as I wanted,
but I can't!'

'Hurry up son, you'll be late for school!'
'It's okay, it stays open all day!'

'I wouldn't want to be in your shoes tomorrow son!'
'Why?'
'They'd be too small for me!'

'What do you think of our new shaving foam?' asked the barber.
'It's the worst I've ever tasted!'

TOMB INSCRIPTIONS
A philosopher: Here I lie, but is it I?
A gardener: Planted spring 1999.
A doctor: A fine doctor once, now never better!
An historian: The past caught up with him.
A fisherman: He has earned his plaice in heaven.
May his sole rest in peace.
Man killed by bear: The victim of a grizzly crime.
Another farmer: Outstanding in his field.

'A camel can go a whole week without touching water!' the
teacher told the class.
'So could I if my mother let me!' muttered Johnnie.

'I thought the glass door was open,
but I discovered it was shut when I ran through it,'
claimed a man on his insurance-claim form.

A man appeared in court recently on a charge of stealing
several string instruments from a music store. He was found
guilty and sentenced to six months' imprisonment.
The newspaper headline the following day read,
'Man Sentenced to Six Months in Violin Case'.

'The death rate in Britain has changed
over the last twenty years,' the teacher told her class.
'How can that be?' asked one girl,
'Surely it's still one death per person?'

'I've already asked you not to eat chocolate in class
and now I find you chewing gum!' shouted the exasperated
teacher. 'Give me an explanation Johnnie.'
'I've finished all the chocolate Miss.'

What happened when the maths teacher died?
He left behind his family and a small sum in his will.

What is a molecule?
A one-eyed spectacule.

What is a magnet?
A wiggly thing you find in an apple.

What is the opposite of woe?
Gee-up!

What is an autobiography?
The life story of a car

What's a monster's favourite colour?
Terror-cotta.

Why did the zombie go to bed early?
Because he was dead on his feet.

In which part of a town do zombies live?
The dead centre.

What do you call a toothless fruit bat?
A fruit gum.

What happens when zombies go skydiving?
They land dead on the target.

Why do ghosts never take a bath?
It dampens their spirits.

What makes young dinosaurs good school pupils?
They always pass with an extinction.

'This is a great day to eat al fresco,' said the first cannibal.
'How does Al feel about it?' asked his friend

What do dinosaurs eat for breakfast?
Tricera-pops.

What song can a man sing to his tie?
I've got you under my chin.

'I've just been stung by a wasp!'
'You'd better put some cream on it straight away.'
'I can't do that, it'll be miles away by now!'

Woman: 'Are my car tyres flat?'
Man: 'No, just at the bottom.'

Why did the man drive his car into the river?
Because a policeman had told him to
dip his headlights.

Where do monsters like to eat?
At a beastro.

Did you hear about the thirsty
boy from Vancouver?
He drank Canada Dry.

'Can I have a day return for
Florence please?' said the
man at the railway station
'But Florence is in Italy sir,'
replied the assistant
'No she isn't, she's standing
over there.'

Did you hear about Gypsy
Rose Lee's new crystal ball?
It cost her a fortune.

What did the frog say when he took his latest book back to
the library?
Reddit, reddit, reddit.

Who is the oldest woman alive?
Anne Tiquity.

Which Roman emperor designed puzzles?
Julius Tessar.

Why don't electricians like to take long
bicycle rides in the country?
They just like to take short circuits.

'Do you see much of your family these days?' Brian asked
his friend the parachutist.
'Yes I manage to drop in on them occasionally.'

What is the disgruntled mountain range in Scotland known as?
The Grumpians.

What did Mary, Queen of Scots choose as her last meal?
A chop.

What makes the old-fashioned sailing ships more
environmentally friendly?
They can cover thousands of miles to the galleon.

Why is Britain always so wet?
Because it has a raining monarch.

Why did the man decide to give up Sumo wrestling?
Because he didn't have the stomach for it anymore.

What do golfers eat for lunch?
A sand wedge.

Why did the woman suggest her husband
should work for the railway?
Because he was such a sound sleeper.

The teacher asked the class to write about an
unusual event that happened during the past week.
Little Johnny got up and read his essay.
It began, 'Daddy fell into the well last week...'

'My goodness!' the teacher exclaimed. 'Is he all right?'
'He must be,' said the boy.
'He stopped yelling for help yesterday.'

'Mummy, Mummy, why has Daddy got so few hairs on his head?' Johnnie asked his mother.
'He thinks a lot,' replied his mother, pleased with herself for coming up with a good answer to her husband's baldness.
'So why do you have so much hair?'

A Texan was taking a taxi tour of London but was in rather a hurry. As they went by the Tower of London the cab driver explained what it was and that construction of it started in 1346 and was completed in 1412. The Texan replied, 'Shoot, a little ol' tower like that? In Houston we'd have that thing up in two weeks!' Next they passed the House of Parliament – started in 1544 and completed in 1618. 'Well boy, we put up a bigger one than that in Dallas and it only took a year!' As they passed Westminster Abbey the cab driver was silent.
'Whoah! What's that over there?' asked the Texan.
The driver replied, 'I don't know, it wasn't there yesterday.'

A man wanted a boat more than anything. His wife kept refusing, but he bought one anyway. 'I'll tell you what,' he told her. 'In the spirit of compromise, why don't you name the boat?' Being a good sport, she accepted. When her husband went to the dock for the maiden voyage, this is the name he saw painted on the side: 'For Sale.'

A woman saw a beautiful tennis bracelet in a jewellery shop window. She went in and asked the assistant if a small deposit would hold it until her husband did something unforgivable.

A cowboy lay sprawled across three entire seats in a posh theatre. When the usher came by and noticed this he whispered to the cowboy, 'Sorry, sir, but you're only allowed one seat.' The cowboy groaned but didn't budge. The usher became more impatient. 'Sir, if you don't get up from there, I'm going to have to call the manager. The cowboy just groaned. The usher marched briskly back up the aisle. In a moment he returned with the manager. Together the two of them tried repeatedly to move the cowboy, but with no success. Finally, they summoned the police, who surveyed the situation briefly then asked, 'All right buddy, what's you're name?'
'Sam,' the cowboy moaned.
'Where you from, Sam?'
With pain in his voice Sam replied, 'The balcony.'

Three cowboys were hanging out in the bunkhouse.
'I know that smart aleck Tex,' said the first.
'He's going to start bragging about that new foreign
car he bought as soon as he gets back.'
'Not Tex,' the second cowboy replied. 'He'll always be just a
good ol' boy. When he walks in, I'm sure he'll just say hello.'
'I know Tex better than either of you,' said the third.
'He's so smart, he'll figure out a way to do both. Here he
comes now.' Tex swung open the bunkhouse door and
shouted, 'Audi, partners!'

The cowboy was trying to buy a health insurance policy. The insurance agent was going down the list of standard questions.
'Ever have an accident?'
'Nope, nary a one.'
'None? You've never had any accidents.'
'Nope. Ain't never had one. Never.'
'Well, you said on this form you were bit by a snake once. Wouldn't you consider that an accident?'
'Heck, no. That dang varmint bit me on purpose.'

The Captain called the Sergeant in. 'Sargeant, I just received a telegram that Private Jones' mother died yesterday. Better go tell him and send him in to see me.' So the Sergeant calls for his morning formation and lines up all the troops. 'Listen up, men,' says the Sergeant. 'Johnson, report to the mess hall for KP. Smith, report to Personnel to sign some papers. Oh by the way, Jones, your mother died, report to the Commanding Officer.'
Later that day the Captain called the Sergeant into his office. 'Hey, Sargeant, that was a pretty cold way to inform Jones his mother died. Couldn't you be a bit more tactful, next time?'
'Yes, sir,' answered the Sarge. A few months later, the Captain called the Sergeant in again with, 'Sargeant, I just got a telegram that Private McGrath's mother died. You'd better go tell him and send him in to see me. This time be more tactful.' So the Sergeant calls his men together. 'Ok, men, everybody with a mother, take two steps forward. Not so fast, McGrath!'

First soldier: 'Pass me the chocolate pudding, would you?'
Second soldier: 'No way, Jose!'
First soldier: 'Why ever not?'
Second soldier: 'It's against regulations to help another soldier to dessert!'

A young naval student was being put through his
paces by an old sea captain. 'What would you do
if a sudden storm sprang up on the starboard?'
'Throw out an anchor, sir,' the student replied.
'What would you do if another storm sprang up aft?'
'Throw out another anchor, sir.'
'And if another terrific storm sprang up forward, what
would you do then?' asked the captain.
'Throw out another anchor, sir.'
'Hold on,' said the officer.
'Where are you getting all those anchors from?'
'From the same place you're getting your storms, sir.'

The officer saw the results of Private Gibson's shooting exercise
and his face fell. The Private exclaimed, 'Sir, I think I am
going to commit suicide by shooting myself.'
'By shooting?' asked the officer, 'Not a bad idea! But take as
many cartridges as possible.'

'Granddad, when you were in the army and were posted as
sentry at night, were you afraid?'
'I was, son, but only until I fell asleep.'

Private Milton went to psychiatrist and complained,
'I have an inferiority complex.'
'Nothing I can do for you', said the doctor. 'In the Army,
Privates don't have an inferiority complex, they're just inferior.'

I have a friend who is a pilot on a 747.
I said 'Hi Jack.' He shot me.

'Daddy, are caterpillars good to eat?' asked Billy
'Have I not told you we don't talk about such things during
meals! Why did you say that? Why did you ask the question?
'It's because I saw one on your lettuce, but now it's gone.'

A lady was picking through the frozen turkeys at the supermarket, but couldn't find one big enough for her family. She asked the young male assistant,
'Do these turkeys get any bigger?'
'No ma'am, they're dead.' He replied.

Two friends were standing in line at a fast-food restaurant, waiting to place our order. There was a big sign posted. 'No notes larger than £20 will be accepted.' The woman in front of them, pointing to the sign, remarked, 'Believe me, if I had a note larger than £20, I wouldn't be eating here.'

A man visits his aunt in the nursing home, but she's asleep so he just sits down in a chair, flicks through a few magazines, and munches on some peanuts sitting in a bowl on the table. Eventually, the aunt wakes up, 'I'm so sorry, Auntie, I've eaten all of your peanuts!'
'That's okay, dear,' the aunt replied. 'After I've sucked the chocolate off, I don't care for them anyway.'

It had been snowing for hours when an announcement came over the university intercom: 'Will students please move their cars so that we can clear the snow.'
Twenty minutes later there was another announcement:
'Will the nine hundred students who went to move fourteen cars please return to class.'

The children had all been photographed, and the teacher was trying to persuade them each to buy a copy of the group picture. 'Just think how nice it will be to look at it when you are all grown up and say, "There's Jennifer; she's a lawyer," or "That's Michael, he's a doctor."'
A small voice from the back of the room rang out, 'And there's the teacher; she's still old, nasty, and wrinkled.'

A pizza delivery boy arrived at the house of a man with a
reputation for being mean. The man asked,
'What is the usual tip?'
'Well,' replied the boy, 'this is my first trip here, but the other
boys reckon if I get fifty pence out of you, I'll be doing well.'
'Is that so?' snorted the man. 'Well, just to show them how
wrong they are, here's three pound.'
'Thanks,' replied the boy, 'I'll put this in my school fund.'
'What are you studying in school?' asked the man.
The lad smiled and said, 'Applied psychology'.

On the way home from the first day of
school, the father asked his son, 'What
did you do at school today?'
The little boy shrugged his shoulders
and said, 'Nothing'.
Hoping to draw his son into
conversation, the father persisted and
said, 'Well, did you learn about any
numbers, study certain letters, or
maybe a particular colour?'
The perplexed child looked at
his father and said, 'Daddy,
didn't you go to school when you
were a little boy?'

'What is the axis of the Earth?' asked the teacher.
'The axis of the Earth is an imaginary line that
passes from one pole to the other, and on which
the Earth revolves,' replied one boy.
'Very good. Now, could you hang clothes on that line?'
asked the teacher.
'Yes.'
'Really, and what sort of clothes?
'Imaginary clothes.'

A man is driving down a country road, when he spots a farmer standing in the middle of a huge field of grass. He pulls the car over to the side of the road and notices that the farmer is just standing there, doing nothing, looking at nothing. The man gets out of the car, walks all the way out to the farmer and asks him, 'Ah excuse me mister, but what are you doing?' The farmer replies, 'I'm trying to win a Nobel Prize.'
'How?' asks the man, puzzled.
'Well, I heard they give the Nobel Prize to people who are out standing in their field.'

A farmer was milking his cow. He was just starting to get a good rhythm going when a bug flew into the barn and started circling his head. Suddenly, the bug flew into the cow's ear. The farmer didn't think much about it, until the bug squirted out into his bucket. It went in one ear and out the udder.

A Texan farmer goes to Australia for a holiday. There he meets an Aussie farmer and gets talking. The Aussie shows off his big wheat field and the Texan says, 'Oh! We have wheat fields that are at least twice as large'. Then they walk around the ranch a little and the Aussie shows off his herd of cattle. The Texan immediately says, 'We have longhorns that are at least twice as large as your cows'. The conversation has, meanwhile, almost died when the Texan sees a herd of kangaroos hopping through the field. He asks, 'And what are those'? The Aussie asks with an incredulous look, 'Don't you have any grasshoppers in Texas'?

There were three men who died, and before God would let them into heaven, he gave them a chance to come back as anything they wanted. The first man said, 'I want to come back as myself, but 100 times smarter. So God made him 100 times smarter. The second man said, 'I want to be better than that guy, make me 1,000 times smarter. So God made him 1,000 times smarter. The last man decided he would be the best. So he said 'God, make me better than both of them, make me 1,000,000 times smarter. So God made him a woman.

A hunter visited another hunter and was given a tour of his home and noticed a stuffed lion.
The visiting hunter asked, 'When did you bag him?'
The host said, 'That was three years ago,
when I went hunting with my wife.'
'What's he stuffed with,' asked the visiting hunter.
'My wife.'

Two friends rented a boat and fished in a lake every day. One day they caught 30 fish. One man said to his friend, 'Mark this spot so that we can come back here again tomorrow.' The next day, when they were driving to rent the boat, the same man asked his friend, 'Did you mark that spot?' His friend replied, 'Yeah, I put a big 'X' on the bottom of the boat.' The first one said, 'You stupid fool! What if we don't get that same boat today!'

Sherlock Holmes and Doctor Watson were on a camping trip. They had gone to bed and were lying there looking up at the sky. Holmes said, 'Watson, look up. What do you see?
'Well, I see thousands of stars.'
'And what does that mean to you?'
'Well, I guess it means we will have another nice day tomorrow. What does it mean to you, Holmes?'
'To me, it means someone has stolen our tent.'

Two young men were out in the woods on a camping trip, when they came upon this great trout brook. They stayed there all day, enjoying the fishing. At the end of the day, knowing

that they would be graduating from college soon,
they vowed that they would meet, in 20 years,
at the same place and renew the experience.
Twenty years later, they met and travelled to a spot near
where they had been years before. They walked into the woods
and before long came upon a brook. One of the men said to
the other, 'This is the place!' The other replied, 'No, it's not!'
The first man said, 'Yes, I recognize the clover growing on the
bank on the other side.' To which the other man replied,
'Silly, you can't tell a brook by its clover.'

**Two hunters were out one day when one hunter fainted.
The other hunter didn't know what to do, so he called 999.
When the person answered the hunter told them that his
partner was dead. The person on the other end tld him to
calm down and make sure the man was really dead.
There was a gunshot and the hunter came back on the line.
He said, 'OK he's dead for sure. What do I do now?'**

Two friends are out hunting deer.
The first man says, 'Did you see that?'
'No,'
'Well, a bald eagle just flew overhead.'
'Oh,' says the second man. A couple of minutes later, the first
man says, 'Did you see that?'
'See what?'
'Are you blind? There was a big, black bear walking on that
hill, over there.'
'Oh.'
A few minutes later the first man says, 'Did you see that?'
By now, the second man is getting aggravated, so he says,
'Yes, I did!'
And the first man says, 'Then why did you step in it?'

A fisherman returned to shore with a giant fish that was bigger and heavier than he. On the way to the cleaning shed, he ran into a second fisherman who had a large net with a dozen baby minnows. The second fisherman looked at the big fish, turned to the first fisherman and said, 'Only caught one, eh?'

A young woman was taking an afternoon nap. When she woke up, she told her husband, 'I just dreamed that you gave me a pearl necklace for Valentine's Day. What do you think it means?'
'You'll know tonight,' he said.
That evening, the man came home with a small package and gave it to his wife. Delighted, she opened it – only to find a book entitled *The Meaning of Dreams*.

'Doctor I'm gaining a huge amount of weight. My stomach is getting really big.'
'You should diet.'
'Really, what colour?'

'I thought you were trying to get into shape?'
'I am. The shape I've selected is a circle.'

A lifeguard told a mother to make her young son stop urinating in the pool. 'Everyone knows,' the mother lectured him, 'that from time to time, young children will urinate in a pool.'
'Oh really?' said the lifeguard. 'From the diving board?'

'I'm afraid I have some very bad news and some good news for you?' said the doctor to the hospital patient. 'I'm afraid we had to amputate both your legs after the accident.'
'Oh no, that's terrible! What's the good news?'
'The man in the next ward has made a super offer on your slippers.'

As the doctor completed an examination of the patient,
he said, 'I can't find a cause for your complaint. Frankly, I
think it's due to drinking.'
'In that case,' said the patient,
'I'll come back when you're sober'

Doctor, doctor, there's a man in the waiting room with a glass
eye named Brown. What does he call the other eye?

Patient: 'I have yellow teeth, what do I do?'
Dentist: 'Wear a brown tie!'

A doctor and a nurse were called to the scene of an accident.
Doctor: 'We need to get these people to a hospital now!'
Nurse: 'What is it?'
Doctor: 'It's a big building with a lot of doctors, but that's not
important now!'

Mrs Smith: 'Help me, doctor! My son, John, swallowed the
can opener!'
Doctor: 'Don't panic. He'll be fine.'
Mrs. Smith: 'But how do I open the can of beans? The toast
is getting cold!'

David: 'My wife beats me, doctor.'
Doctor: 'Oh dear. How often?'
David: 'Every time we play Scrabble!'

A patient shook his doctor's hand in gratitude and said,
'Since we are the best of friends, I would not want to insult
you by offering payment. But I would like you to know that
I have mentioned you in my will.'
'That is very kind of you,' said the doctor emotionally, and
then added, 'Can I see that prescription I just gave you?
I'd like to make a little change.'

A man, after being hurt, calls 999 for help.
Man: 'Operator, operator, call me an ambulance!'
Operator: 'Okay, sir, you're an ambulance!'

A man enters a barbershop for a shave. While the barber is
foaming him up, he mentions the problems he has getting a
close shave around the cheeks. 'I have just the thing,' says
the barber taking a small wooden ball from a nearby drawer.
'Just place this between your cheek and gum.' The client
places the ball in his mouth and the barber proceeds with
the closest shave the man has ever experienced. After a few
strokes the client asks in garbled speech.
'And what if I swallow it?'
'No problem,' says the barber. 'Just bring it back tomorrow
like everyone else does.'

A man and a little boy entered a barbershop together.
After the man received the full treatment – shave, shampoo,
manicure, haircut, etc. – he placed the boy in the chair.
'I'm going to buy a green tie to wear for the parade,' he said.
'I'll be back in a few minutes.'
When the boy's haircut was completed and the man still
hadn't returned, the barber said, 'Looks like your daddy's
forgotten all about you.'
'That wasn't my daddy,' said the boy. 'He just walked up, took
me by the hand and said, "Come on, son, we're going get a
free haircut!"'

In the supermarket was a man pushing a trolley, which
contained a screaming, bellowing baby. The gentleman kept
repeating softly, 'Don't get excited, Albert; don't scream,
Albert; don't yell, Albert; keep calm, Albert.'
A woman standing next to him said, 'You certainly are to be
commended for trying to soothe your son.'
The man looked at her and said, 'No, I'm Albert.'

A woman spent most of her holiday sunbathing on the roof of her hotel. She wore a bathing suit the first day, but on the second, she decided that no one could see her up there, and she slipped out of it for an overall tan. Suddenly she heard someone running up the stairs. She was lying on her stomach, so she just pulled a towel over her rear. 'Excuse me, miss,' said the flustered assistant manager of the hotel, 'We don't mind your sunbathing on the roof, but we would very much appreciate your wearing a bathing suit as you did yesterday'.
'What difference does it make?' the woman asked calmly.
'No one can see me up here.'
'Not exactly,' said the embarrassed man. 'You're lying on the dining-room skylight.'

On opening his new shop, a man received a bouquet of flowers. He became dismayed on reading the enclosed card, which said 'Deepest Sympathy'. While puzzling over the message, his telephone rang. It was the florist, apologizing for having sent the wrong card. 'Oh, it's all right,' said the man. 'I'm a businessman and I understand how these things can happen.'
'But,' said the florist, 'I accidentally sent your card to the funeral party.'
'Well, what did it say?' ask the storekeeper.
'"Congratulations on your new location",' came the reply.

A wise schoolteacher sends this note to all parents on the first day of school: 'If you promise not to believe everything your child says happens at school, I'll promise not to believe everything he says happens at home.'

What's brown, smelly and sounds like a bell?
Duuung.

A Sunday-school teacher asked her class why Joseph and Mary took Jesus with them to Jerusalem. A small child replied, 'They couldn't get a baby-sitter.'

A very dirty little fellow came in from playing in the garden and asked his mother, 'Who am I?'
Ready to play the game she said, 'I don't know!
Who are you?'
'WOW!' cried the child. 'Mrs Farman was right! She said I was so dirty, my own mother wouldn't recognize me!'

An ant and an elephant share a night of romance.
The following morning the elephant is dead.
'Oh no,' says the ant. 'One night of romance and now I'll be spending the rest of my life digging a grave!'

A dog thinks, 'Hey, these people I live with feed me, love me, provide me with a nice warm, dry house, pet me, and take good care of me... They must be Gods!'
A cat thinks: 'Hey, these people I live with feed me, love me, provide me with a nice warm, dry house, pet me, and take good care of me... I must be a God!'

What's the hardest thing about learning to ride a bicycle?
The ground.

Two rabbits were being chased by a pack of wolves.
After a minute or two, one rabbit turns to the other and says, 'Do you want to make a run for it or stay here until we can outnumber them?'

I used to be a werewolf, but I'm okay nooooooooowwww.

Q: Does an elephant ever forget?
A: Only if you loan him money.

Q: What sound does a grape make when an elephant steps on it?
A: It just lets out a little wine.
What's a duck's favourite television show?
The feather forecast.

Two cows were standing in a pasture.
A young bull came by and said, 'Good morning ladies'.
One of the cows said, 'Mooooo!' The second cow thought to
herself, 'Damn! I was going to say that.'

There are two fish in a tank, and one fish asks the other,
'How do you drive this thing?'

A horse walks into a bar and the barman says,
'Why the long face?'

**Q: Why does the elephant
wear pink tennis shoes?
A: They don't make
white in his size.**

Q: Why is the
elephant floating down
the river on his back
with all four legs sticking
up in the air?
A: So he won't get his
pink tennis
shoes wet.

Q: Why is the elephant wearing three pink tennis shoes
and one yellow one?
A: He didn't lift his leg
high enough.

Three vampires walk into a bar and sit down.
The first vampire says, 'I'd like a pint of blood'.
The second vampire says, 'I'd like a pint of blood, too'.
Then the third vampire says, 'I'd like a pint of plasma'.
Then the barman says, 'Okay, so let me get this straight,
you want two bloods and a blood light?'

A string walks into a bar and asks the waiter for a beer.
The waiter says, 'I am sorry but we can't serve strings here'.
The string goes home and ties himself in a knot.
He goes back to the bar about an hour later,
sits down and says, 'Waiter, give me a beer'.
The waiter says, 'Hey aren't you the string who
came in here earlier?'
The string replies, 'No, I'm a frayed knot'.

How many Pentium designers does it take
to screw in a light bulb?
1.99904274017, but that's close enough
for non-technical people.

A man walks into a bar and asks the barman for a drink.
Then he asks for another. After a couple more drinks, the
barman gets worried. 'What's the matter?' the barman asks.
'My wife and I had a fight,' explained the man, 'and now she
isn't talking to me for a whole thirty-one days.'
The barman thought about this for a while. 'But, isn't it a
good thing that she isn't talking to you?'
'Yeah, except today is the last night.'

A physics professor was explaining a particularly complicated concept to his class when a pre-med student interrupted him. 'Why do we have to learn this stuff?' he blurted out. 'To save lives,' the professor responded, before continuing the lecture. A few minutes later the student spoke up again. 'So how does physics save lives?' The professor stared at the student without saying a word. 'Physics saves lives,' he finally continued, 'because it keeps the idiots out of medical school.'

The doctor took Dan into the room and said, 'Dan, I have some good news and some bad news.' 'Oh, no. Give me the good news, I guess,' Dan replied. 'They're going to name a disease after you.'

Why did the nurse go to art school?
To learn how to draw blood.

**Why did the mirror cross the road?
To see itself.**

Do you like my new jacket?
It's great. Shame your body doesn't suit it, though.

**I never forget a face, but in your case
I'll make an exception!**

She has a pretty little head – for a head, it's pretty little.

**He says he has a mind of his own.
He's welcome to it – who else would want it?**

He should study to be a bone specialist – he has the head for it.

**Oh my God! What's that big ugly thing on your neck?
Oh, it's just your head.**

Your family is so poor, when I went to your house
I stepped on a cigarette and your Daddy shouted,
'Hey, who turned off the heater?'

**Knock, knock!
Who's there?
George Washington!
George Washington who?
George Washington who? Didn't you learn anything in
history class?**

A man is driving home from work when he sees a crazy man
driving on the wrong side of the road. He remembered his
grandmother was out driving so he phoned her to tell her
about the crazy driver. 'Grandma, watch out for
a crazy driver on the wrong side of the road.'
'One? There's hundreds!'

**What type of shoes do plumbers wear?
Clogs.**

A man and his wife are driving along when the wife turns to
her husband and says, 'I want a divorce. I've been having an
affair with your best friend for two years now, and he wants me
to move in with him. I want the kids, the house, the car, the
boat, all the money, and the pets. Is there anything you want?'
'No,' he says as he slams his foot on the accelerator and steers
the car directly towards a concrete pole. 'That's all right –
I've got the airbag.'

**In winter why do we try to keep the house as warm as it was
in summer when we complained about the heat?**

Why do banks charge a fee on 'insufficient funds' when they know there is not enough?
Why do they use sterilized needles for death by lethal injection?

Why do Kamikaze pilots wear helmets?

Whose idea was it to put an 's' in the word 'lisp'?

Why is it that no matter what colour bubble bath you use the bubbles are always white?

Why do people keep running over a string a dozen times with their vacuum cleaner, then reach down, pick it up, examine it, then put it down to give the vacuum one more chance?

When we are in the supermarket and someone rams our ankle with a shopping trolley then apologizes for doing so, why do we say, 'It's all right'? Well, it isn't all right so why don't we say, 'That hurt, you clumsy idiot?'

So the judge said to me, 'You threw your wife out of a 17th-storey window. What do you have to say for yourself?'
I said, 'We just moved from the ground floor. I forgot.'

Two men were leaving church on a bright Sunday morning.
'You know,' said the first friend, 'I can always tell who the golfers are in church.'
'How's that?' asked his friend.
'It's easy,' he said. 'Just look at who is praying with an interlocking grip.'

Q: What's the difference between a golfer and a fisherman?
A: When a golfer lies he doesn't have to bring anything
home to prove it!

Q: What are the four worst
words you could
hear during a round of golf?
A: It's still your turn!

**Why do black widow spiders
kill their males after mating?
To stop the snoring before it
starts.**

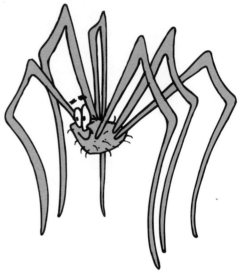

One elderly couple is visiting
another for supper.
The two women go into the
kitchen for a moment,
leaving the men to talk. One
of the men says to the other, 'The missus and I went to the
nicest restaurant last night.'
'Is that right?' the other enquires. 'What was it called?'
'That's just it,' he replies 'I can't recall. What's the name of
that red flower that has thorns all over it?'
'A rose?' he responds.
'Yeah, that's it,' he says energetically.
He then whirls around and yells into the kitchen, 'Hey, Rose!
What was the name of that restaurant we went to last night?'

**Why is divorce so expensive?
Because it's worth it.**

A banker is someone who lends you an umbrella
when the Sun is shining, and who then asks for it
back again when it starts to rain.

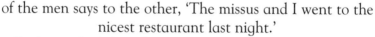

He has one of those mighty minds – mighty empty.

He has a one-track mind, and the traffic on it is very light.

**A bargain is something you don't need
at a price you can't resist.**

A bicycle can't stand on its own because it's two-tyred.

**Don't get married. Find a woman you hate and buy her a
house. It's a lot easier on you.**

Is reading on the toilet considered multi-tasking?
Seen it all. Done it all. Can't remember most of it.

Sometimes women are overly suspicious of their husbands.
When Adam stayed out very late for a few nights, Eve became
upset. 'You're running around with other women,' she charged.
'You're being unreasonable,' Adam responded. 'You're the only
woman on Earth.' The quarrel continued until Adam fell
asleep, only to be awakened by someone poking him in the
chest. It was Eve.
'What do you think you're doing?' Adam demanded.
'Counting your ribs!'

**After God had created Adam he noticed that he
looked very lonely. He decided to help.
He said 'Adam, I've decided to make you a woman.
She'll love you, cook for you, be sweet to you,
and understand you.'
Adam said 'Great! How much will she cost me?'
The answer came back, 'An arm and a leg'.
'Well,' said Adam, 'what can I get for a rib?'**

What did God say after She made Eve?
Practise makes perfect.

**What did God say after creating Adam?
I can do better.**

A family of moles had been hibernating all winter. One
beautiful spring morning, they woke up. The father mole stuck
his head out of the hole and looked around.
'Mother Mole!' He called back down the hole. 'Come up here!
I smell honey, fresh-made honey!'
The mother mole ran up and squeezed in next to him.
'That's not honey, that's maple syrup! I smell maple syrup!'
The baby mole, still down in the hole, was sulking. 'I can't
smell anything down here but molasses.'

**How do you make a cat go 'woof'?
Soak it in petrol and throw it on fire.**

What did one lab rat say to the other?
'I've got my scientist so well trained that every time I push the
buzzer, he brings me a snack.'

Old software engineers never die, they just log out.

What toy hates to be touched?
Lego!

**A man runs into a bank holding a twig aloft.
'This is a stick up,' he cries.
'So what?' says the bank clerk, placing a log on the desk in
front of her. 'This is a major branch.'**

'Darling what did you do before you met me?'
'Anything I wanted.'

Noah was standing at the gangplank, checking off the pairs
of animals, when he saw three camels trying to get on board.
'Wait a minute!' said Noah. 'Two each is the limit.
One of you will have to stay behind.'
'It won't be me,' said the first camel. 'I'm the camel whose
back is broken by the last straw.'
'I'm the one people swallow while straining at a gnat,'
said the second.
'I,' said the third, 'am the one that shall pass through the eye
of a needle sooner than a rich man shall enter Heaven.'
'Come on in,' said Noah.
'The world is going to need all of you!'

A little boy got lost at the YMCA and found himself in the
women's locker room. When he was spotted, the room burst
into shrieks, with ladies grabbing towels and running for cover.
The little boy watched in amazement and then asked,
'What's the matter – haven't you ever seen a little boy before?'

One day, three men were hiking and unexpectedly came
upon a raging river. They needed to get to the other side,
but had no idea of how to do so. The first man prayed,
saying, 'Please God, give me the strength to cross this river'.
Poof! God gave him big arms and strong legs, and he was
able to swim across the river in about two hours. Seeing
this, the second man prayed to God, saying, 'Please God,
give me the strength and the tools to cross this river'. Poof!
God gave him a rowboat and he was able to row across the
river in about an hour, after almost capsizing the boat.
The third man had seen how this worked out for the other
two, so he also prayed to God saying, 'Please God, give me

the strength and the tools ... and the intelligence ... to cross
this river.' And poof! God turned him into a woman.
She looked at the map, hiked upstream a couple
of hundred yards then walked across the bridge.

The Japanese authorities have stopped all live animal
movements following the discovery of a number of nibbled beds
in the Tokyo area.
They fear it may be the start of an outbreak of Futon Mouse.

A Scotsman was visiting a friend in the mountains of
Canada. The first morning in the cabin, he awoke and stood
by the window admiring the scenery. Suddenly, he noticed a
huge animal walk by. 'Och, whut's thaaat?' he said.
His Canadian friend looked out and said,
'Oh, that's a moose.'
'Och! If thaaat's a moose, hoo big are your
cats aroond here?'

On their anniversary night, a husband sat his wife down in the
den with her favourite magazine, turned on the soft reading
lamp, slipped off her shoes, patted and propped her feet and
announced that he was preparing dinner all by himself.
'How romantic!' she thought. Two-and-a-half hours later,
she was still waiting for dinner to be served. She tiptoed to the
kitchen and found it a colossal mess.
Her harried husband, removing something indescribable
from the smoking oven, saw her in the doorway.
'Almost ready!' he vowed. 'Sorry it took me so long –
I had to refill the pepper shaker.'
'Why, honey, how long could that have taken you?'
'More than an hour, I reckon. Wasn't easy stuffing it through
those tiny little holes.'

What's the difference between a used-car salesman
and a software salesmen?
Only the used-car salesman
knows when he lying.

Old software engineers never die,
they just reboot.

In days past,
children were given
names that sound
strange to us today –
Prudence, Charity,
Faith, and so on. One boy
was named Amazing, and he resented it all his life.
People laughed at him because of it. He told his wife that,
when the time came, he did not want his name on his
tombstone. When he died, she followed his wishes and put
on the tombstone, 'Here lies a man who was faithful to his
wife for 60 years'. But even in death, he couldn't escape the
curse, because everyone that looked at his tombstone said,
'Why, that's Amazing!'

A man was seen fleeing down the hall of the hospital just
before his operation. 'What's the matter?' he was asked.
He said, 'I heard the nurse say, "It's a very simple operation,
don't worry, I'm sure it will be all right".'
'She was just trying to comfort you,
what's so frightening about that?'
'She wasn't talking to me. She was talking to the doctor!'

If at first you don't succeed, destroy all evidence that you tried.

Everyone has a photographic memory,
some just don't have the film.

**Three-year-old Nick was especially fond of his grandfather.
When he died, Nick's mother explained to him that his
grandfather had gone to Heaven.
'Mum, Grandpa is with God, right?' Nick asked.
'Yes,' his mother replied.
'Well, why doesn't God fix him and send him back?'**

A young man was talking to God.
'How long is a million years to You?' he asked.
'A million years to Me is like a single second to you,'
God replied.
'How much is a million dollars to You?' the young man asked.
'A million dollars to Me is like a penny to you,' God replied.
'In that case,' the young man ventured,
'Could I have one of Your pennies?'
'Certainly, My Son,' God replied. 'Just a second.'

**'Doctor, I'm so depressed and lonely. I don't have any
friends, no one will come near me, and everybody
laughs at me. Can you help me accept my ugliness?'
'I'm sure I can.' the psychiatrist replied. 'Just go over and lie
face down on that couch.'**

A couple of old men were golfing when one said he was going
to Dr Taylor for a new set of dentures in the morning.
His friend remarked that he had gone to the
same dentist a few years before.
'Is that so?' the first said. 'Did he do a good job?'
'Well, I was on the course yesterday when the fellow on the
ninth hole hooked a shot,' he said. 'The ball must have been
going 200 mph when it hit me in the stomach. That,' he
added, 'was the first time in two years my teeth didn't hurt.'

Visiting their grandmother's house, two young boys were saying their prayers at bedtime. The younger boy started loudly shouting his prayers: 'God, please send me a Nintendo ... and a new bike!'
'Why are you shouting your prayers?' his older brother asked. 'God isn't deaf.'
'No, but Grandma almost is!' the little brother answered.

I work in a busy office where a computer going down causes quite an inconvenience. Recently one of our computers not only crashed, it made a noise that sounded like a heart monitor. 'This computer has flat-lined,' a co-worker called out with mock horror.
'Does anyone here know how to do mouse-to-mouse?'

An office reports that they have an answering machine that instructs callers to leave their name and address, and to spell any difficult words. Early one Monday, when the secretary was reviewing the weekend messages, she heard an enthusiastic young woman recite her name and address and then confidently offer, 'My difficult word is reconciliation. R-E-C-O-N-C-I-L-I-A-T-I-O-N.'

Some men find a man lying on the sidewalk. They assume that the old man is drunk, so they decide to be good Samaritans and get him home. They pick him up off the pavement, and drag him out the door. On the way to the car, he falls down three times. He tells them where he lives and when they arrive at his house, they help him out of the car and he falls down four more times. They ring the bell, and one of the men says to the woman who answers, 'Here's your husband!'
The man's wife says,
'Well, where in the world is his wheelchair?'

When Mrs Jones died, she went to St Peter and asked about
her husband who had died several years earlier.
'What was his name?' St Peter asked.
'Harry Jones,' she replied.
'There are so many here with that name,
what else can you tell me?' asked St Peter.
'Well,' she answered, 'The last thing he said before he died
was that if I were ever unfaithful to him, he would turn over
in his grave.'
'Ah!' said St Peter, 'You're looking for Pinwheel Harry!'

On a foggy night at sea, a ship's captain saw what appeared to
be the lights of another ship heading toward him.
He instructed his signalman to contact the other ship
by signal light. He sent the message,
'Change your course ten degrees to the north.'
The reply came, 'Change YOUR course
ten degrees to the south!'
The captain responded, 'I am a Captain.
Change YOUR course ten degrees
to the north.'
Reply: 'I am a Seaman First Class.
You change YOUR course ten
degrees to the south.'
The captain was furious. He had
his signalman reply, 'I am a
battleship! YOU change your
course ten degrees to the
north.'
Reply: 'I am a
lighthouse! You change
YOUR course ten
degrees to the south!'

A businessman had a tiring day on the road. He checked into a hotel and, because he was concerned that the dining room might close soon, left his luggage in the left luggage and went immediately to eat. After a leisurely dinner, he reclaimed his luggage and realized that he had forgotten his room number. He went back to the desk and told the clerk on duty, 'My name is George Smith. Could you please tell me what room I am in?' 'Certainly,' said the clerk. 'You're in the lobby.'

The teacher asked little Johnny, 'If your father earned £100,000 and gave half of it to your mother, what would she have?' Little Johnny replied, 'A heart attack'.

As soon as she had finished convent school, a bright young girl named Lena shook the dust of Ireland off her shoes and made her way to New York where, before long, she became a successful performer in showbusiness. Eventually she returned to her hometown for a visit and on a Saturday night went to confession in the church where she had always attended as a child. In the confessional Father Sullivan recognized her and began asking her about her work. She explained that she was an acrobatic dancer, and he wanted to know what that meant. She said she would be happy to show him the kind of thing she did on stage. She stepped out of the confessional and within sight of Father Sullivan she went into a series of cartwheels, leaping splits, handsprings and back flips. Kneeling near the confessional, waiting their turn, were two middle-aged ladies. They witnessed Lena's acrobatics with wide eyes, and one said to the other, 'Will you just look at the penance Father Sullivan is giving out this night, and me without me bloomers on!'

One day as Mr and Mrs Fisher were sleeping, an intruder entered their house. The intruder put a knife to the neck of the woman and said, 'I like to know the names of my victims before I kill them. Wwhat is your name?'
'My name is Elizabeth,' the woman replied.
The intruder said, 'You remind me of my mother who was also named Elizabeth, so I can't kill you.'
The intruder then turned to the husband and asked, 'What is your name?'
'My name's Phillip, but my friends, well ... they call me Elizabeth.'

Mrs Smith likes sitting in the park and feeding the pigeons. One day she took a whole loaf of fresh bread just to feed her daily company. Little by little she fed each pigeon with joy. She sat there without being noticed by anyone when suddenly a man started to shout that she shouldn't throw away good food on a bunch of pigeons that can find food anywhere when there are people starving in other countries. Mrs Smith said in anger, 'Well, I can't throw that far!'

Little Bobby was spending the weekend with his grandmother after a particularly trying week in playschool. His grandmother decided to take him to the park on Saturday morning. It had been snowing all night and everything was beautiful.
His grandmother remarked, 'Doesn't it look like an artist painted this scenery? Did you know God painted this just for you?'
Bobby said, 'Yes, God did it and He did it left-handed.'
This confused his grandmother a bit, and she asked him, 'What makes you say God did this with his left hand?'
'Well,' said Bobby, 'we learned at Sunday School last week that Jesus sits on God's right hand!'

A boss was complaining in our staff meeting the other day that he wasn't getting any respect. Later that morning he went to a local card and novelty shop and bought a small sign that read, 'I'm the Boss'. He then taped it to his office door. Later that day when he returned from lunch, he found that someone had taped a note to the sign that said, 'Your wife called. She wants her sign back!'

When the employees of a restaurant attended a fire-safety seminar, they watched a fire official demonstrate the proper way to operate an extinguisher. 'Pull the pin like a hand grenade,' he explained, 'then depress the trigger to release the foam.' Later an employee was selected to extinguish a controlled fire in the parking lot. In her nervousness, she forgot to pull the pin. The instructor hinted, 'Like a hand grenade, remember?' In a burst of confidence she pulled the pin – and hurled the extinguisher at the blaze.

Two elderly ladies were discussing their husbands over tea. 'I do wish that my George would stop biting his nails. He makes me terribly nervous.'
'My Billy used to do the same thing,' the older woman replied. 'But I broke him of the habit.'
'How?'
'I hid his teeth.'

My friend was on duty in the main computer lab on a quiet afternoon, when he noticed a young woman sitting in front of one of the workstations with her arms crossed across her chest, staring at the screen. After about 15 minutes she was still in the same position, only now she was impatiently tapping her foot. Finally, he approached her and asked if she needed help. She replied, 'Yes, it says "press ANY button", but I can't find it!'

In a class on abnormal psychology, the instructor was about to introduce the subject of manic depression. He asked, 'How would you diagnose a patient who walks back and forth, screaming at the top of his lungs one minute, then sits in a chair weeping uncontrollably the next?' A young man in the rear raised his hand and suggested earnestly, 'A football coach?'
'I couldn't repair your brakes, so I made your horn louder,' said the mechanic

What do you get if you cross a Pointer with a Setter? A poinsettia for Christmas.

Bill woke up one morning, and made his way to the front door to get the newspaper. After opening the door, he reached down for the paper and saw a snail lying on the porch.
Bill picked up the snail and threw it across the street.
Two years later, on a Sunday morning, Bill was going through his same routine. Wake up, put on slippers and a dressing gown, and make his way to the front door to retrieve the paper. When he opened the door, there sat a snail. The snail looked up at Bill and said, 'Now, was that REALLY necessary?'

I tried bareback riding once – but I fell off the horse.

Why did the actor travel to the Wild West?
To find a stagecoach.

A man is lying on the road, dazed, after being hit by a bus. He hears a voice above him, 'Don't worry sir, I'll look after you, I'm a professional.'
'Doctor?'
'No, undertaker.'

Three friends die in a car accident and they go to an orientation in Heaven. They are all asked, 'When you are in your casket and friends and family are mourning you, what would you like to hear them say about you?'
The first guy says, 'I would like to hear them say that I was a great doctor in my time and a great family man.'
The second guy says, 'I would like to hear that I was a wonderful husband and a schoolteacher who made a huge difference in our children of tomorrow.'
The last guy replies, 'I'd like to hear them say, "Look! He's moving!"'

Why did the monkey fall out of the tree?
Because it was dead.

A waiter asks a man, 'May I take your order, sir?'
'Yes,' the man replies. 'I'm just wondering, exactly how do you prepare your chickens?'
'Nothing special, sir. We just tell them straight out that they're going to die.'

You can't buy love,
but you certainly can pay dearly for it.

REJECTED GREETING CARDS
'Looking back over the years that we've been together,
I can't help but wonder: What was I thinking?'
**'Congratulations on your wedding day!
Too bad no one likes your wife.'**
'How could two people as beautiful
as you have such an ugly baby?'

MORE REJECTED GREETING CARDS
**'I've always wanted to have someone to hold, someone to
love. After having met you, I've changed my mind.'**
'I must admit, you brought Religion in my life.
I never believed in Hell until I met you.'
**'As the days go by, I think of how lucky I am that you're not
here to ruin it for me.'**

EVEN MORE REJECTED GREETING CARDS
'As you grow older, Mum, I think of all the gifts you've given
me, like the need for therapy.'
**'Thanks for being a part of my life! I never knew what evil
was before this!'**
'Before you go, I would like you to take this knife out of my
back. You'll probably need it again.'
'Someday I hope to get married, but not to you.'
'You look great for your age. Almost lifelike!'
**'When we were together, you always said you'd die for me.
Now that we've broken up,
I think it's time you kept your promise.'**

A FINAL ATTEMPT TO GET THE
GREETING CARDS PRINTED
**'Congratulations on your new bundle of joy.
Did you ever find out who the father was?'**

'I'm so miserable without you. It's almost like you're here.'

'You are such a good friend that if we were on a sinking ship and there was only one life jacket. I'd miss you heaps and think of you often.'

An archaeologist is a best husband a woman can have. As older she gets, the more interested he is in her.

A fine is a tax for doing wrong.
A tax is a fine for doing well.

I love being married. It's so great to find that special person you want to annoy for the rest of your life.

I wear my wife's glasses because she wants me to see things her way.

A good friend will bail you out of jail.
A great friend will be in the cell next to you saying, 'Damn, that was fun!'

Can a teacher give a homeless man homework?

At age 4, success is not peeing in your pants.
At age 12, success is having friends.
At age 20, success is having sex.
At age 35, success is making money.
At age 70, success is having sex.
At age 80, success is having friends.
At age 90, success is not peeing your pants.

Why does sour cream have an expiry date?

Marriage means that someone helps you cope with all the problems you never had when you were a bachelor.

**My wife ran away with my best friend.
To tell you the truth, I really miss him.**

The more I know people – the more I like my dog.

**Be nice to your children.
They are the ones who choose
your old people's home.**

Why do we wash bath towels?
Aren't we clean when we
use them?

**How come
abbreviated is
such a long
word?**

When cheese gets
it's picture taken,
what does it say?

**What would a chair
look like,
if your knees bent the
other way?**

There was this guy at a bar, just looking at his drink. He stays
like that for half of an hour. Then, this big trouble-making
truck driver steps next to him, takes the drink from the guy,
and just drinks it all down. The poor man starts crying.
The truck driver says, 'Come on man, I was just joking. Here,
I'll buy you another drink. I just can't stand to see a man cry.'
'No, it's not that. This day is the worst of my life. First, I fall

asleep, and I go late to my office. My boss fires me. When I leave the building, to my car, I found out it was stolen. The police said that they could do nothing. I get a cab to return home, and when I leave it, I remember I left my wallet and credit cards there. The cab driver just drives away. I go home, and when I get there, I find my wife in bed with the gardener. I leave home, and come to this bar. And just when I was thinking about putting an end to my life, you show up and drink my poison.'

**A man was telling his neighbour,
'I just bought a new hearing aid. It cost me four thousand pounds, but it's state of the art. It's perfect.'
'Really,' answered the neighbour. 'What kind is it?'
'Twelve thirty.'**

At the height of a political corruption trial, the prosecuting attorney attacked a witness. 'Isn't it true,' he bellowed, 'that you accepted five thousand pounds to compromise this case?' The witness stared out the window, as though he hadn't heard the question.
'Isn't it true that you accepted five thousand pounds to compromise this case?' the lawyer repeated loudly.
The witness still did not respond.
Finally, the judge leaned over and said,
'Sir, please answer the question.'
'Oh,' the startled witness said, 'I thought he was talking to you.'

**While he is on a business trip, a husband sends a telegram to his wife. 'I wish you were here,' it reads.
The message received by wife was 'I wish you were her.'**

A wife with near maturing pregnancy goes to railway station to return to her husband. At the reservation counter, when her turn came, it was the last ticket. Taking pity on a very old lady next to her in the queue, she offered her berth to the old lady and sent a telegram to her husband which reached him as: 'Shall be coming tomorrow, heavy rush in the train, gave birth to an old lady.'

While touring a small South American country, a woman was shown a bullfight. The guide told her, 'This is our number one sport.'
The horrified woman said, 'Isn't that revolting?'
'No,' the guide replied. 'Revolting is our number two sport.'

A site foreman had 10 very lazy men working for him, so one day he decided to trick them into doing some work for a change. 'I've got a really easy job today for the laziest one among you,' he announced. 'Will the laziest man please put his hand up?' Nine hands went up.
'Why didn't you put your hand up?' he asked the tenth man.
'Too much trouble,' came the reply.

A carpet layer had just finished installing carpet for a lady. He stepped out for a smoke, only to realize he'd lost his cigarettes. In the middle of the room, under the carpet, was a bump. 'No sense pulling up the entire floor for one pack of cigarettes,' he said to himself. He proceeded to get out his hammer and flattened the hump.
As he was cleaning up, the lady came in. 'Here,' she said, handling him his pack of cigarettes.
'I found them in the hallway.'
'Now,' she said, 'if only I could find my parakeet.'

A man managed to burn both ears,
so they were asking him at the hospital how it happened.
He said, 'I was ironing my clothing and the phone rang, so
instead of the phone I picked up the iron and burned my ear.'
'But how on Earth did you burn the other ear?'
the doctor asked.
'How do you think I called you people?'

SIGNS YOU ARE GETTING OLD
You find yourself listening to talk radio.
You daughter says she got pierced and you look at her ears.
The pattern on your trousers and on the sofa match.

MORE SIGNS YOU ARE GETTING OLD
You turn down free tickets to a rock concert because you have
to work the next day.
**You call the police on a noisy party next door instead of
grabbing beer and joining it.**
When jogging is something you do to your memory.

EVEN MORE SIGNS YOU ARE GETTING OLD
**You remember the 'Rolling Stones'
as a rock group not a corporation.**
All the cars behind you flash their headlights.
**You bought your first car for the same amount
you paid for your son's new trainers.**

FINAL SIGNS YOU ARE GETTING OLD
You don't know how to operate a fax machine.
You actually ASK for your father's advice.
When someone mentions SURFING you picture waves
and a surfboard.

How would you describe an old, lost, runaway dog?
Over the hill and fur away.

Why did the cowboy go skydiving?
He wanted a chute out.

What do little birdies see
when they get knocked unconscious?

What do you do when you see an endangered animal
eating an endangered plant?

What's the name of the world's fattest puppet?
Mr Paunch.

How do you stop a runaway elephant?
With a trunkuillizeer.

What do you call a pheasant with blonde feathers?
Fair game.

What's the name of the most selfish girl in the world?
Mimi.

Why did the ballet dancers go to the pub?
To do their exercises at the bar.

When is a question like a fishing net?
When it's got a catch.

What did the electrician, turned gymnast, specialize in?
Volting.

Why did the girl not want to throw a ball at the fair?
She was coconut shy.

Why is the pen mightier than the sword?
Because nobody has invented the ballpoint sword.

Did you hear about the fly that landed on the cow's head?
It went in one ear and out the udder.

**Who has a parrot that
shouts 'pieces of four'?
Short John Silver.**

What did the duck do after
he'd eaten his
lunch in the restaurant?
Asked for his bill.

**Why did the man take four
baths every day?
Because his doctor had told
him to take his pills in
water.**

My wife has only got two
faults:
everything she says and
everything she does.

**Where is Felixstowe?
At the end of his foot.**

Where can you never win a
soccer match?
Thailand.

Why do journalists meet in ice-cream parlours?
They hope to get a big scoop.

What happened to the biscuit that fell into the cement mixer?
It became a tough cookie.

**What do you get if you cross
a sound system with a typewriter?
Stereotype.**

Yesterday a charity football match organized by the Royal
family was cancelled.
It was reigned off.

**How did the plumber help to get the meal ready?
He drained the vegetables.**

What happens to dead robots?
They rust in pieces.

**What do fridge and freezer engineers do in their spare time?
They chill out.**

What do watchmakers do in their spare time?
They unwind.

**What do thieves do in their spare time?
Take it easy.**

What do racing drivers do in their spare time?
Slow down.

**What do lawyers do in their spare time?
Go courting.**

How does a cricketer get a girlfriend?
He bowls a maiden over.

Why do models get married so often?
They are pro-posers.

Since my wife's taken up gardening she's really gone to seed.

Since my wife's taken up sewing she's had me in stitches
every night.

Since my son has taken up skateboarding he's really flipped.

What cars do dolphins drive?
Multi-porpoise vehicles.

How do you stop a cockerel from crowing?
Pop him in the oven the night before.

What do you get if you cross a panda with a harp?
A bear faced lyre.

Why did the man without a mouth go to Holland?
To get tulips from Amsterdam.

What's the difference between a church bell and a thief?
One peels from the steeple and the other
steals from the people.

What's the difference between a hungry man and a greedy man?
A hungry man longs to eat and a greedy man eats too long.

Why is the sea restless?
Because it's got stones in its bed.

Which animals can go without food for the longest?
Stuffed ones.

**What has a million ears but can't hear?
A cornfield.**

What's used one day and made the next?
A bed.

**What's the similarity between a builder and a makeup artist?
They both need a good foundation to work on.**

Who invented King Arthur's round table?
Sir Cumference.

**Which king of England invented the fireplace?
Alfred the Grate.**

Which king of England invented the apple box?
Alfred the Crate.

**Which king of England was a chiropodist?
William the Corn Curer.**

What was the name of the comedian that
tried to conquer the world?
Attila the Pun.

**Who succeeded the first Prime Minister of England?
The second one.**

What do you get if you cross a dog with a computer?
A creature that retrieves joysticks.

Why are bakers the best-paid professionals in the world?
Because they've got more dough.

What do you call a millionaire that never washes himself?
Filthy rich.

If pandas live on bamboo shoots, what do polar bears live on?
Ice.

Did you hear about the artist that became an actor and
managed to draw a large crowd at the theatre?

Did you hear about the man that always wore white at night
so cars could see him?
A snowplough knocked him down.

How do you make an antidote?
Be really nice to her when she comes to see you.

I knew someone who thought Hertz Van Rental
was a Dutch painter.

What's the difference between a doormat
and a bottle of cough mixture?
One's taken up and shaken, the other is shaken up and taken.

Did you hear the joke about the bed?
It hasn't been made up yet.

What did the vicar say to the sprig of mint?
Go in peas.

Did you hear about the man who just slept in his boxers?
He had a vestless night.

I used to play percussion, but I couldn't drum up any enthusiasm for it.

What's round and dangerous?
A vicious circle.

Did you hear about the latest invention to see through even the thickest of walls?
They've called it a window.

Did you hear about the man who wrote a poem first thing in the morning, as soon as he got up?
He went from bed to verse.

Did you hear about the egg in the monastery?
It went out of the frying pan and into the friar.

What's black and white and bounces?
A zebra on a trampoline.

What's another thing that is black and white and bounces?
A nun on a pogo stick.

What's yet another thing that's black and white and bounces?
A rubber penguin.

What's the difference between a black cloud
and someone with toothache?
One pours with rain and the other roars with pain.

What word is always spelled badly?
Badly.

What is a water otter?
A kettle.
What is a buttress?
A female goat.

What happened to the shy stone?
In time it grew to become a little boulder.

How do you make a lamb stew?
Keep it waiting.

Did you hear the sad story of the unfortunate archaeologist?
He got buried in his work.

What did the successful detective use to carry around his
investigation notes?
An open and shut case.

Why did the carpenter go to the doctor?
Because he had a saw finger.

When is a car driver not a car driver?
When he turns into a side street.

When is a door not a door?
When it is a jar.

Why was the writer kept in prison?
Because he hadn't finished his sentence.

Why are inventors the worse cooks?
Because they're ideas are half-baked.

Why did the policeman arrest the sheep on the motorway?
Because it tried to do a ewe turn.

Can skunks sing?
No, but they can hum.

What has fifty legs and can't walk?
A centipede with a spade through it.

What makes people think that carrots are good for eyesight?
It is rare to see a rabbit wearing glasses.

What lies on the ground, 100 feet up in the air and smells?
A dead centipede.

Why did the Buddhist refuse painkillers during
his root-canal treatment?
He wanted to transcend dental medication.

Why did the bird fall out of the sky?
It was dead.

Why did the jackdaw cross the road?
To crow about its success.

How can you tell if a chicken likes you?
It gives you a peck on the cheek.

What machinery is necessary to move a heavy pig?
A porklift truck.

Why do you always see pigeons at horse racing events?
Because they like to have a flutter.

Did you hear the story about the pigeon
that wanted to buy New York?
He even put a deposit on the Statue of Liberty.

Did you hear the joke about the slippery eel?
No, well you wouldn't grasp it anyway.

Why do dogs smell?
Because they never change their coats.

Did you hear about the man who called his dog carpenter?
He chose the name because it did odd jobs
around the house.

Did you know about the conspiratorial flock of doves?
They decided to stage a coo.

Why is a sofa like a roast chicken?
Because they're both full of stuffing.

What did one fly say to the second fly?
Time to send in the swat team.

How do you stop fish from smelling?
Cut off their noses.

I thought I saw an eye doctor on an Alaskan island, but it turned out to be an optical Aleutian.

'Waiter this coffee tastes like mud.'
'Well it was fresh ground this morning.'

If you eat soup that's nine days old, will you get bad broth?

'Waiter, look at the state of your shirt,
it's covered in jelly and custard!'
'Yes sir, doing this job does get me a trifle messy.'

'Waiter, this food looks delicious but I can't eat it.'
'Why's that sir?'
'You haven't brought me a knife and fork.'

A Sunday school teacher was having a hard time getting her young students to grasp the message of the Good Samaritan. Finally she pointed to one of the children and asked, 'Alison, suppose you passed car park and saw a man in ragged clothes lying on the ground, badly beaten up, covered with blood. What would you do?' The eight-year-old said, 'I think I would be sick.'

A young man asked an old rich man how he made his money. The old guy fingered his worsted wool vest and said, 'Well, son, it was 1932 and I was down to my last penny.
I invested that penny in an apple. I spent the entire day polishing the apple and, at the end of the day, I sold the apple for sixpence. 'The next morning, I invested that sixpence in six apples. I spent the entire day polishing them and sold them for half a crown. I continued this system for a month, by the end of which I'd accumulated a fortune of twelve guineas.
Then my wife's father died and left us two million pounds.'

A British couple have five children. Their names are Roger, Larry, Johnny, Adam, and Ding Kong Wong. They called their fifth child Ding Kong Wong because the survey said that one in five babies are Chinese.

Bankers usually split up with their girlfriends by making a quick withdrawal.

'That boy over there is really annoying me!' said Sadie to her friend in the nightclub.
'But he's not even looking at you!' replied her friend.
'That's why he's annoying me.'

Robinson Crusoe was delighted when an old window washed up on the beach. At least he'd have something to open on his birthday!
What do all the Smiths in the phone book have in common? They all have phones.

I was getting into my car, and this bloke says to me, 'Can you give me a lift?' I said 'Sure, you look great, the world's your oyster, go for it.'

I got home, and the phone was ringing. I picked it up, and said 'Who's speaking please?' And a voice said, 'You are'.

I rang up a local building firm. I said
'I want a skip outside my house.'
He said 'I'm not stopping you.'

I went up into the attic and found a Stradivarius and a Rembrandt. Unfortunately Stradivarius was a terrible painter and Rembrandt made lousy violins.

A policeman stopped me the other night. He tapped on the window of the car and said, 'Would you please blow into this bag, sir'. I said: 'What for, Officer?' He replied, 'My chips are too hot'.

I got stopped again last night by another policeman. He said, 'I'd like to follow you to the nearest police station'. I said 'What For?' He said, 'I've forgotten the way'.

I got into a cab and said to the taxi driver, 'King Arthur's Close'. He said, 'Don't worry, we'll lose him at the next set of lights'.

I went to Blackpool on holiday and knocked at the first boarding house that I came to. A women stuck her head out of an upstairs window and said, 'What do you want?'. 'I'd like to stay here.' 'Ok. Stay there, then.'

I went to the doctor. He said, 'you've got a very serious illness'. I said, 'I want a second opinion'. He said, 'all right – you're ugly as well.'

I went into a pub, and I ate a ploughman's lunch. He was livid.

'Doctor, I can't stop singing the green green grass of home.' 'That sounds like Tom Jones syndrome.' 'Is it common?' 'It's not unusual.'

I rang up my local swimming baths. I said, 'Is that the local swimming baths?' He said 'It depends where you're calling from.'

I went to the butcher's the other day and I bet him 50 quid that he couldn't reach the meat off the top shelf. He replied, 'no, the steaks are too high.'

If you stand in the middle of a library and go 'Aaaaaaagghhhh' everyone just stares at you. But if you do the same thing on an aeroplane, everyone joins in.

Why did Tigger stick his head down the toilet?
He was looking for Pooh.

A man is found guilty of murder and sentenced to death in the electric chair. As part of the execution the man who flips the switch asks the murderer if he has any last requests. With tears in his eyes the murderer says, 'Yes I have. When the switch is flipped, can I hold my defence lawyer's hand?'

What do you call a boomerang that doesn't work?
A stick.

What do you get when you cross a snowman with a vampire?
Frostbite.

What lies at the bottom of the ocean and twitches?
A nervous wreck.

Did you hear about the man who was tap dancing?
He broke his ankle when he fell into the sink.

How do you double the value of a Skoda car?
Fill it with petrol.

One Sunday a vicar told his congregation that the church needed some more money and asked the people to consider giving a little extra in the offering plate. He said that whoever gave the most would be able to pick out three hymns.
After the offering plates were passed, the pastor glanced down and noticed that someone had placed a wad of notes on the plate. He was so excited that he immediately shared his joy with his congregation and said he'd like to personally thank the person who placed the money in the plate.
A very quiet, elderly, saintly lady all the way in the back shyly raised her hand. The vicar asked her to come to the front.
Slowly she made her way to the vicar. He told her how wonderful it was that she gave so much and in thanksgiving asked her to pick out three hymns.
Her eyes brightened as she looked over the congregation, pointed to the three handsomest men in the building and said, 'I'll take him and him and him.'

A funeral service was being held in a church for a woman who had just passed away. At the end of the service, the pallbearers were carrying the casket out when they accidentally bumped into a wall, jarring the casket. They heard a faint moan. They opened the casket and found that the woman was still alive. She lived for 10 more years. A ceremony was held at the same church and at the end of the service the pallbearers were again carrying out the casket.
As they were walking,
the husband cried out, 'Watch out for the wall!'

Eagles may soar, but rabbits don't get sucked into jet engines.

Is depression just anger without enthusiasm?

A customer walks into a post office one day to see a middle-aged, balding man standing at the counter methodically placing 'Love' stamps on bright pink envelopes with hearts all over them. He then takes out a perfume bottle and starts spraying scent all over them. The customer's curiosity gets the better of him and he goes up to the balding man and asks him what he is doing.
'I'm sending out 1,000 Valentine cards signed "Guess who?"'
'But why?' asks the man.
'I'm a divorce lawyer.'

One day a group of husbands and wives went to a scientific programme. The doctor there was showing them brains from real people and telling how expensive it would be to buy one. He said that the male brains were much more expensive than the female ones. The men thought this was becuase they were special, but one of the women asked, 'Why is that, doctor?'
The doctor answered, 'The men's brains cost more because they have never been used'.

Two women were in a hair salon talking about their home lives when the subject of flighty husbands came up.
'It's unbelievable,' one woman said. 'I can never figure out where he goes at night.'
'I know exactly what you mean,' said the other woman. 'One second he's in the house, and the next he's gone without a trace.'
'Well,' said a woman eavesdropping nearby. 'I always know where my husband is.'
'How do you manage that?' the other two asked.
'Easy,' she replies. 'I'm a widow.'

What did one undertaker say to the other?
Pass me another cold one!

How many ears did Davy Crocket have?
His left ear, his right ear and his wild front ear.

As an aeroplane is about to crash, a female passenger
frantically jumps up, removes all her clothing and
announces, 'If I'm going to die,
I want to die feeling like a woman. Is there anyone on this
plane who is man enough?'
A man stands up, removes his shirt and says,
'Here, iron this.'

How do you know when a man's going to say
something intelligent?
He starts his sentence with 'A woman told me...'

Why did the koala bear fall out of the tree?
Because it was dead.

A woman and a man are involved in a car accident. Both of
their cars are totally demolished but amazingly neither of them
is hurt. After they crawl out of their cars, the woman says,
'So you're a man, that's interesting. I'm a woman. Just look at
our cars! There's nothing left, but fortunately we are unhurt.
This must be a sign from God that we should meet and be
friends and live together in peace for the rest of our days.'
Flattered, the man replied, 'Oh yes, I agree with you
completely!'
'This must be a sign from God!' The woman continued, 'And
look at this, here's another miracle. My car is completely
demolished but this bottle of wine didn't break. Surely God
wants us to drink this wine and celebrate our good fortune.'
Then she hands the bottle to the man.

The man nods his head in agreement, opens it and drinks half the bottle and then hands it back to the woman. The woman takes the bottle, immediately puts the cap back on, and hands it back to the man.

The man asks, 'Aren't you having any?'

The woman replies, 'No. I think I'll just wait for the police.'

Gardening expert, Phil Durham, winner of five gold medals for his marrows, gave up growing them as he had developed a hernia. He now grows pumpkins and has already developed a new strain.

A Japanese inventor has succeeded in creating a surgical truss with a built-in calculator. This means that users can count on their own support.

Yesterday Virginia Gold was named 'Worst Cook of the Year' when she burned the tin opener.

Did you hear about the man who lost his left arm and left leg
in a car crash?
He's all right now.

**Why do bagpipers walk while they are playing?
They are trying to get away from the noise.**

I almost had a psychic girlfriend, but she left me before we met.

**We should protect bacteria. They are the only culture some
people have.**

The only substitute for good manners is fast reflexes.

**When things all seem to be coming at you, you're probably
driving the wrong way up a motorway.**

Ambition is a poor excuse for not having the sense to be lazy.

**Yesterday Bruce Wright celebrated 50 years of not
gambling, drinking or womanizing. Unfortunately, he was
involved in a dreadful accident when a truck carrying beer
barrels swerved to avoid two men delivering a slot machine
to massage parlour.**

Clumsy barber, Geoffrey Thompson, was so distraught about
the number of complaints he received that he tried to kill
himself. Fortunately, he tried to cut his own throat and only
succeeded in shaving himself.